AF575974

SHELLS

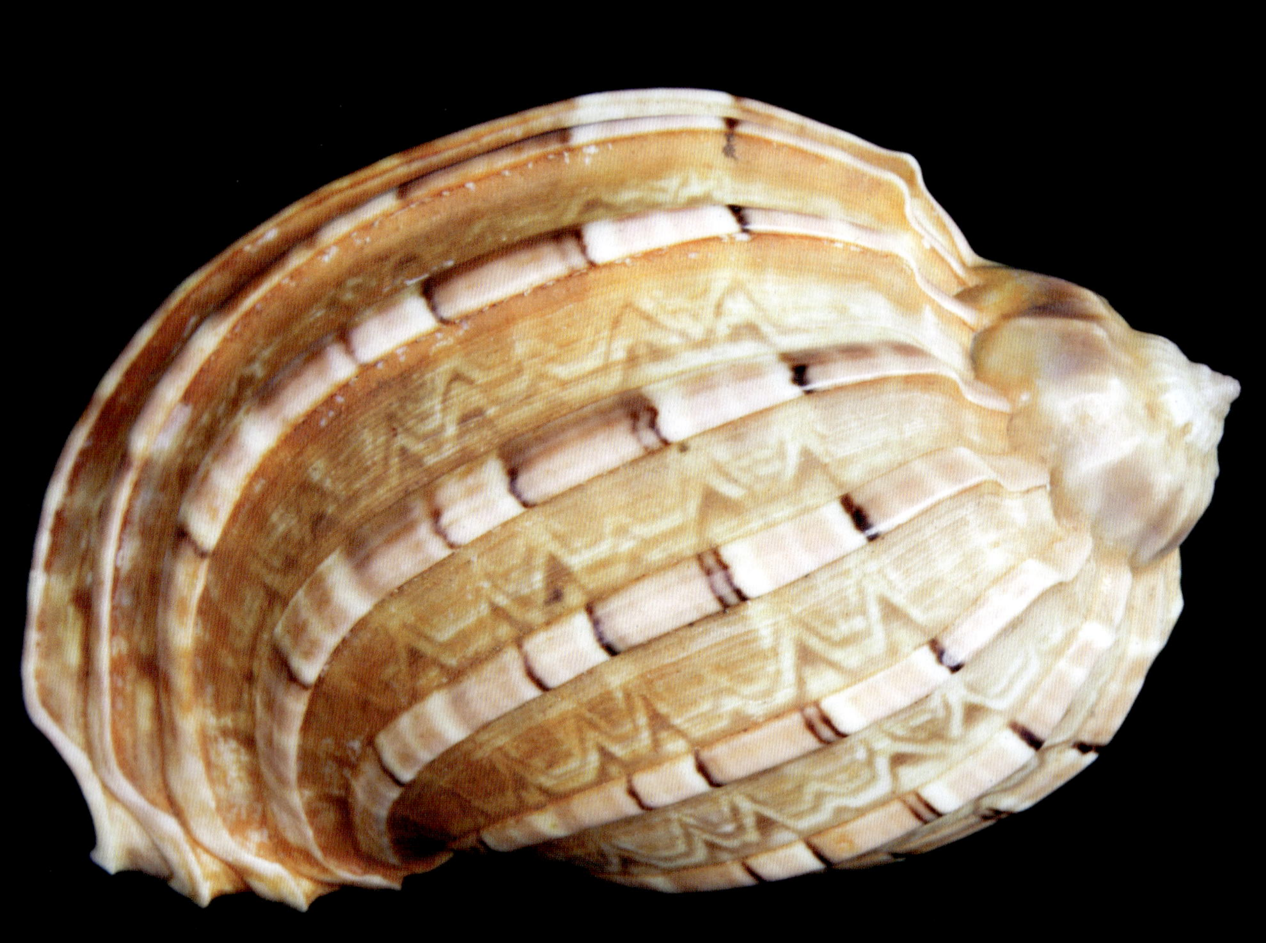

SHELLS

Nature's Exquisite Creations

JOYCE TENNESON

Down East Books

Down East Books
An imprint of The Globe Pequot Publishing Group, Inc.
64 South Main Street
Essex, CT 06426
www.globepequot.com

Copyright © 2011 by Joyce Tenneson
All rights reserved

Design by Miroslaw Jurek

ISBN 978-0-89272-976-0

Library of Congress Cataloging-in-Publication Information available upon request

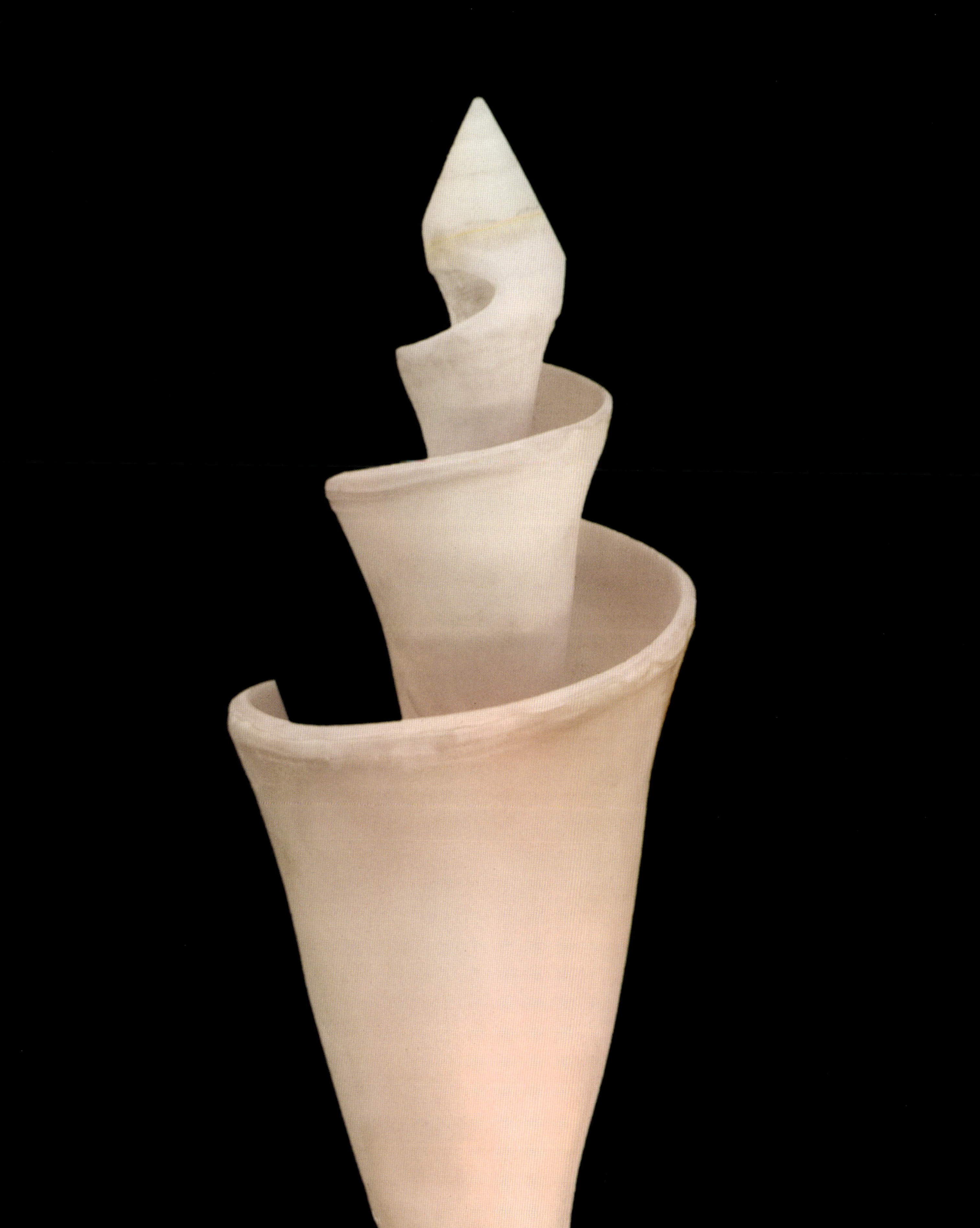

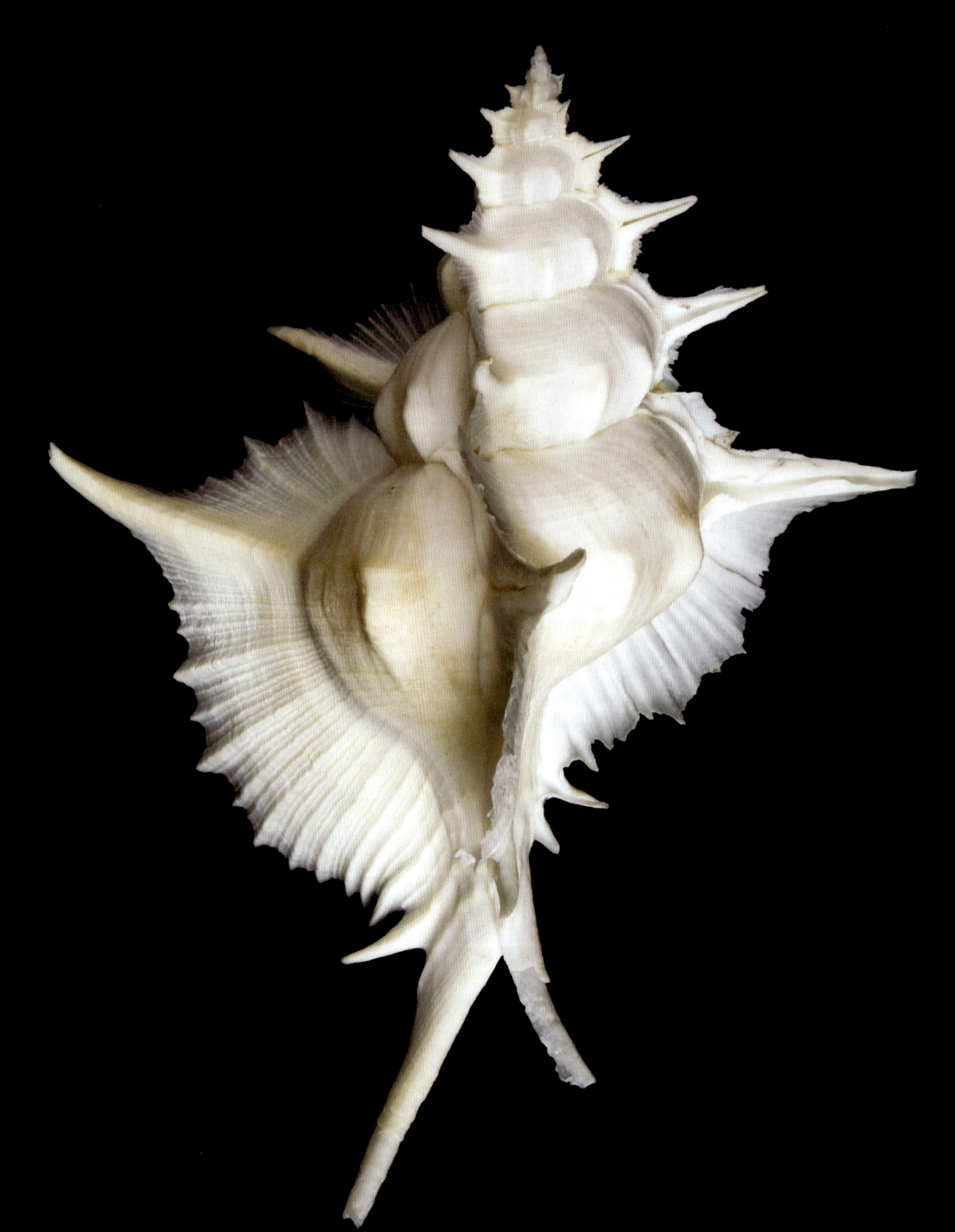

This book is dedicated to my grandchildren:
Ruby, Lucy, Ethan, and Bennett.
Their sense of wonder enriches my life,
and their fresh eyes help me to see
the world in new ways.

Seashells are undeniably some of nature's most exquisite creations. Throughout the ages, poets, kings, shamans, artists, and architects have been fascinated by their form and symbolism. For more than six million years, mollusks have survived by building protective skeletal "homes" in a mesmerizing variety of sizes, shapes, and colors.

Early cultures valued seashells to produce sounds that could contact the gods or spirits, which they believed held special powers. During the Middle Ages and the Renaissance, royalty throughout Europe considered shells to be valuable gifts. Shells were also used as money to purchase goods. In the fifteenth century, Chinese explorers collected shells from India and Africa for their emperor. Monasteries housed their own collections and used them as models for manuscripts and illustrations. Seashells appeared frequently in still life paintings by the Dutch masters, and Leonardo Da Vinci used the common snail as a basis for many of his winding staircase designs.

My own interest in seashells has been one simply of awe. I am drawn to the sensual qualities of shells—the silky curves of the nautilus, the undulating edges of the scallop shell. With this book I hope to inspire the viewer to see seashells in new ways, to look beyond their merely scientific depictions.

A decade ago, I started photographing shells in the studio on a black velvet backdrop, which enhanced their jewel-like presence. Recently, I began to explore shells' more personal essence by photographing them outside on gold backdrops. This has allowed me to examine the essence and more intimate qualities of my subjects. Throughout history, gold has been used as a spiritual element in art. For the Incas, gold symbolized the sun god. Photographing in natural light gives the shells a more radiant appearance, as they take on some of magic of the golden light. I have also been drawn to create small groupings of shells, seeing them as friends or possibly family members, much in the same way that I photograph people.

In the end, our love of seashells is perhaps a reflection of our subconscious awareness that they are symbols of the timeless, vast ocean, in which all life began. They call us back to our own origins, and our longing for beauty and depth.

Joyce Tenneson

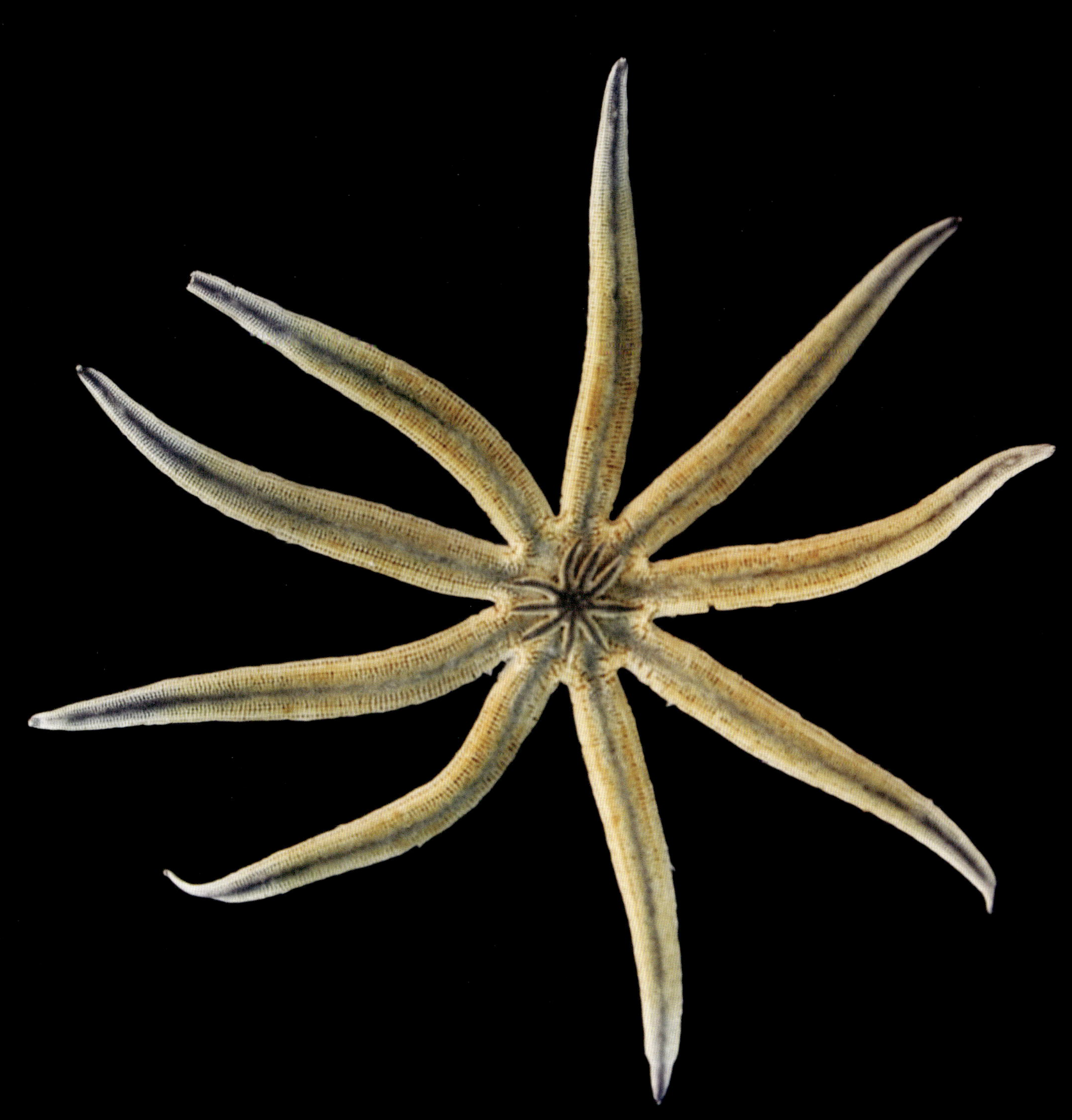

The real voyage of discovery consists not in seeking new landscapes, but in having new eyes.

—Marcel Proust

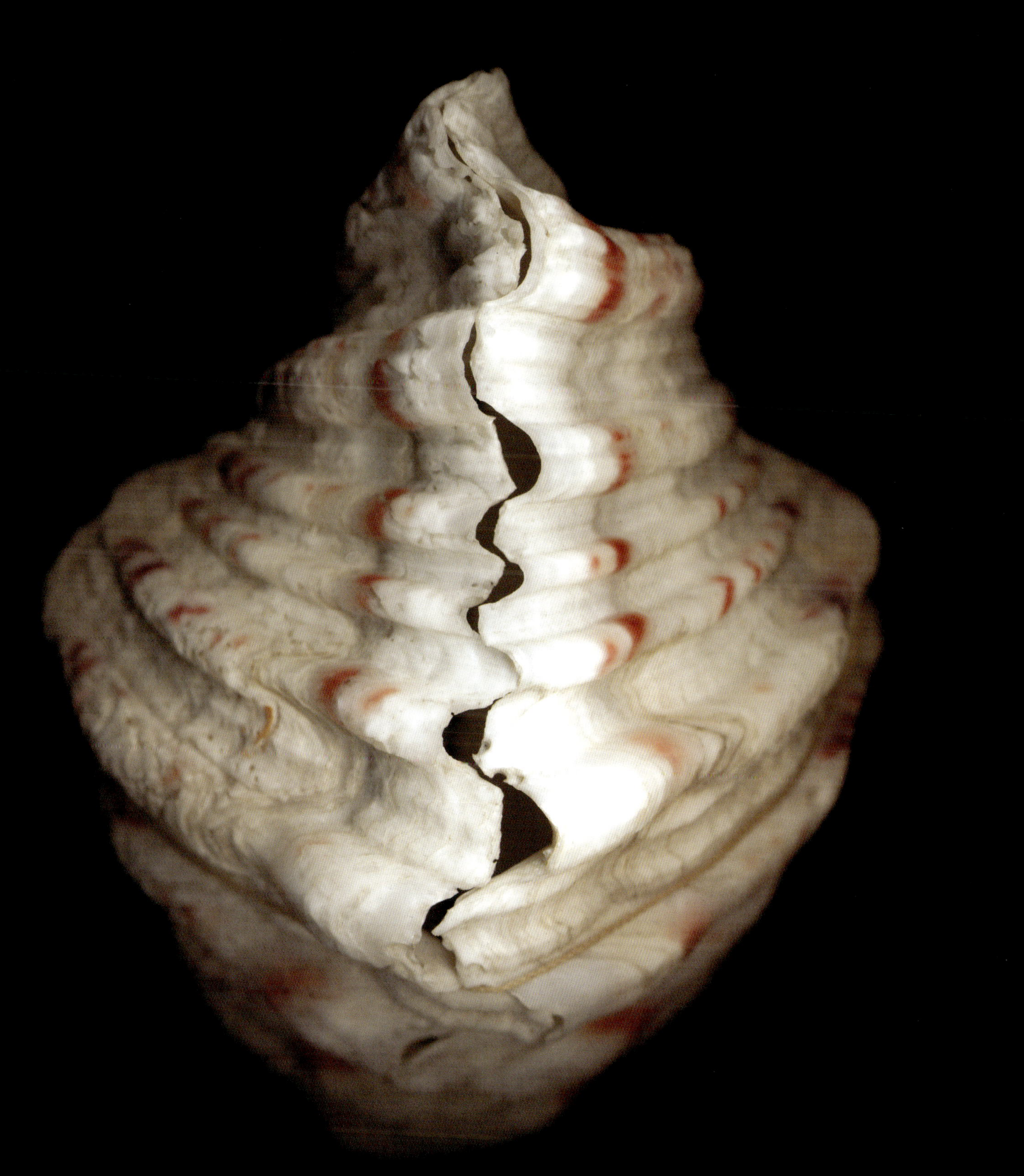

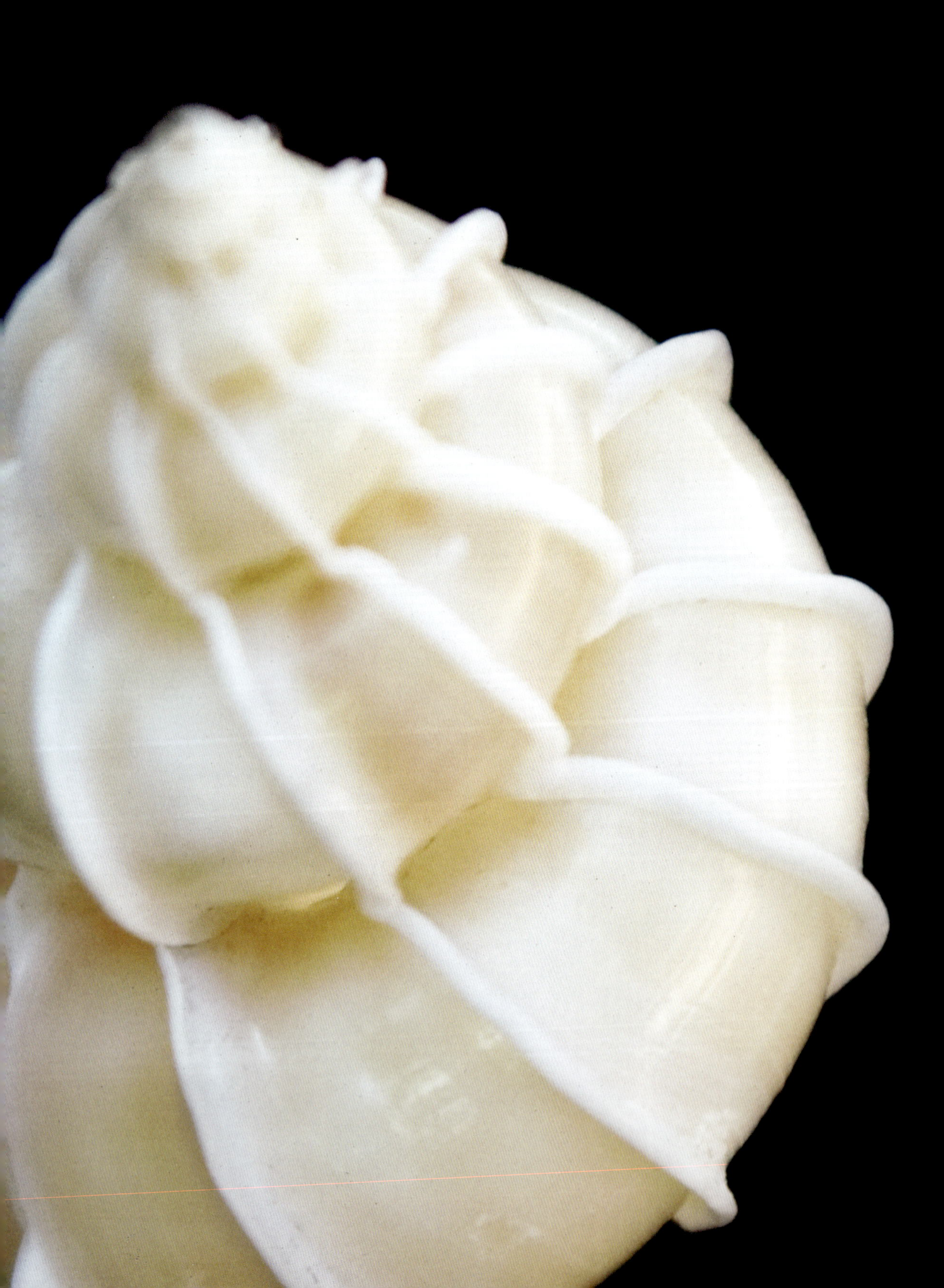

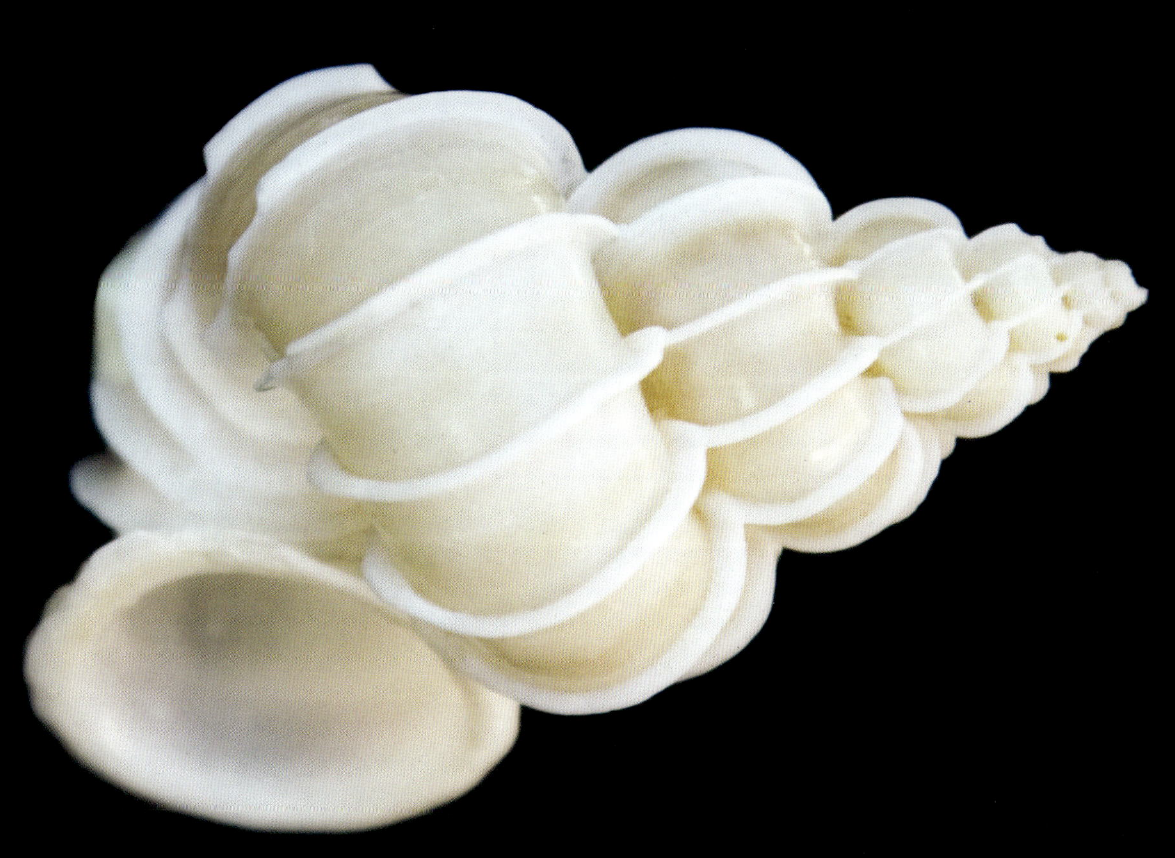

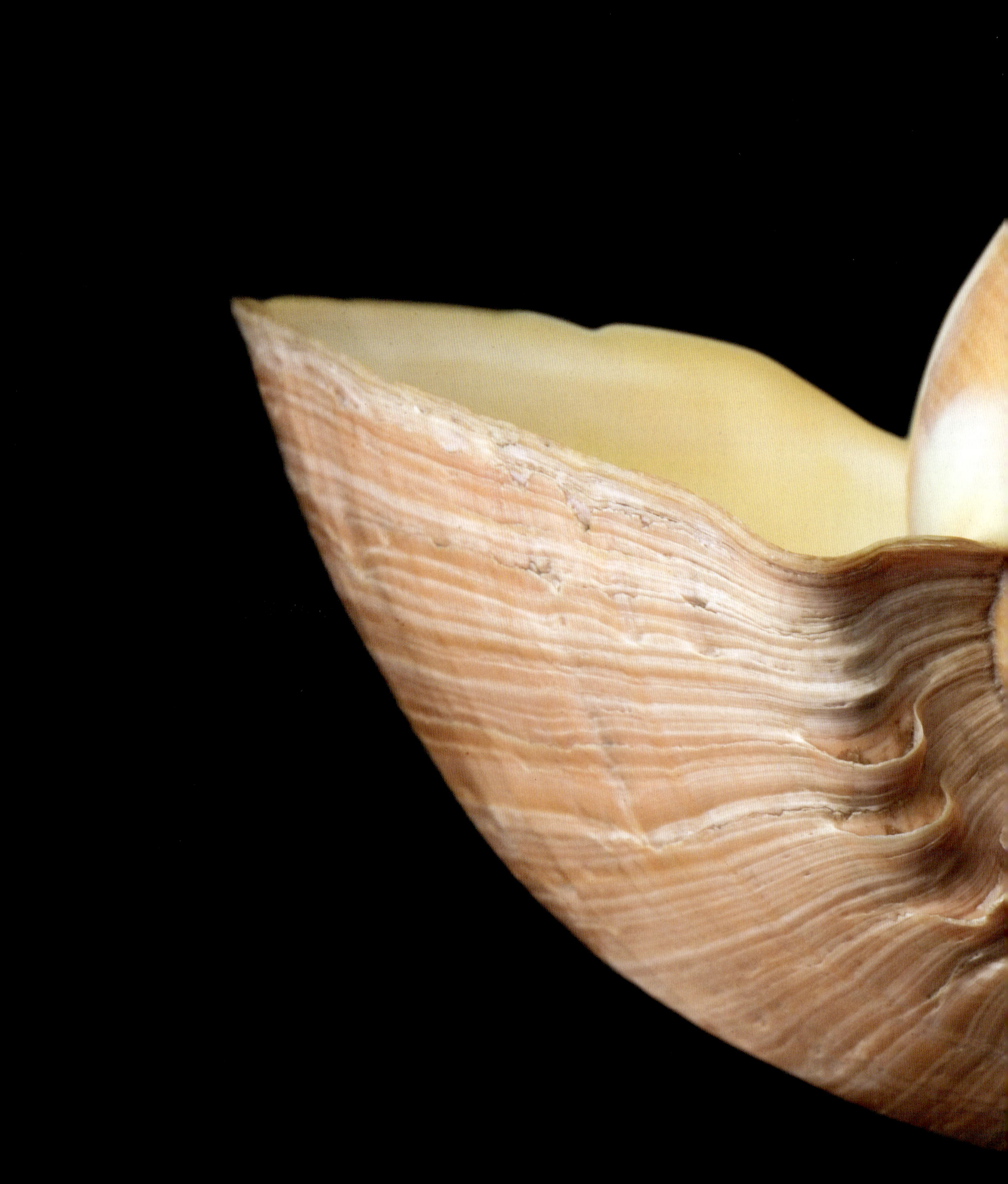

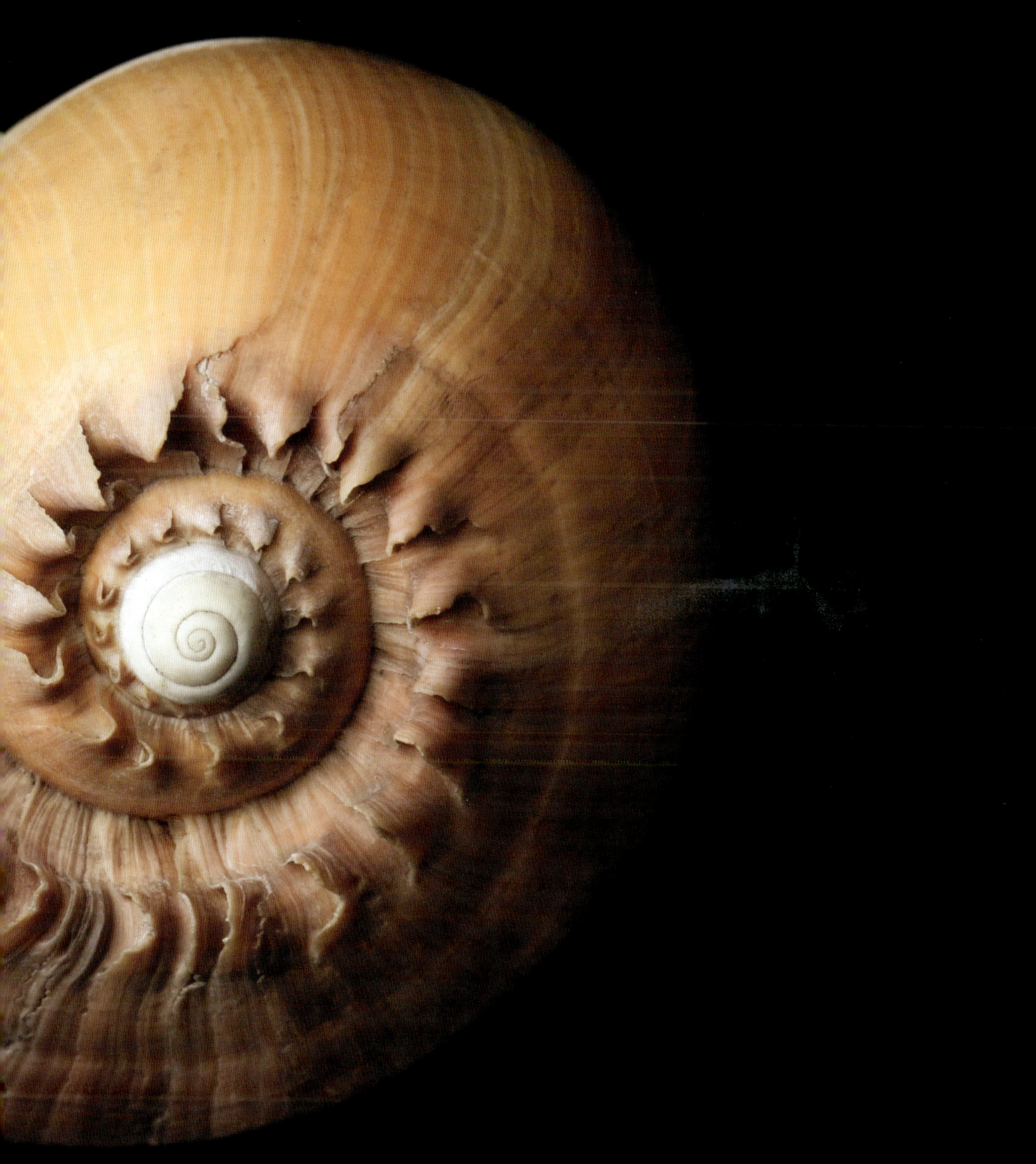

You see things and say, "Why?"; but I dream things that never were and I say, "Why not?"

—George Bernard Shaw

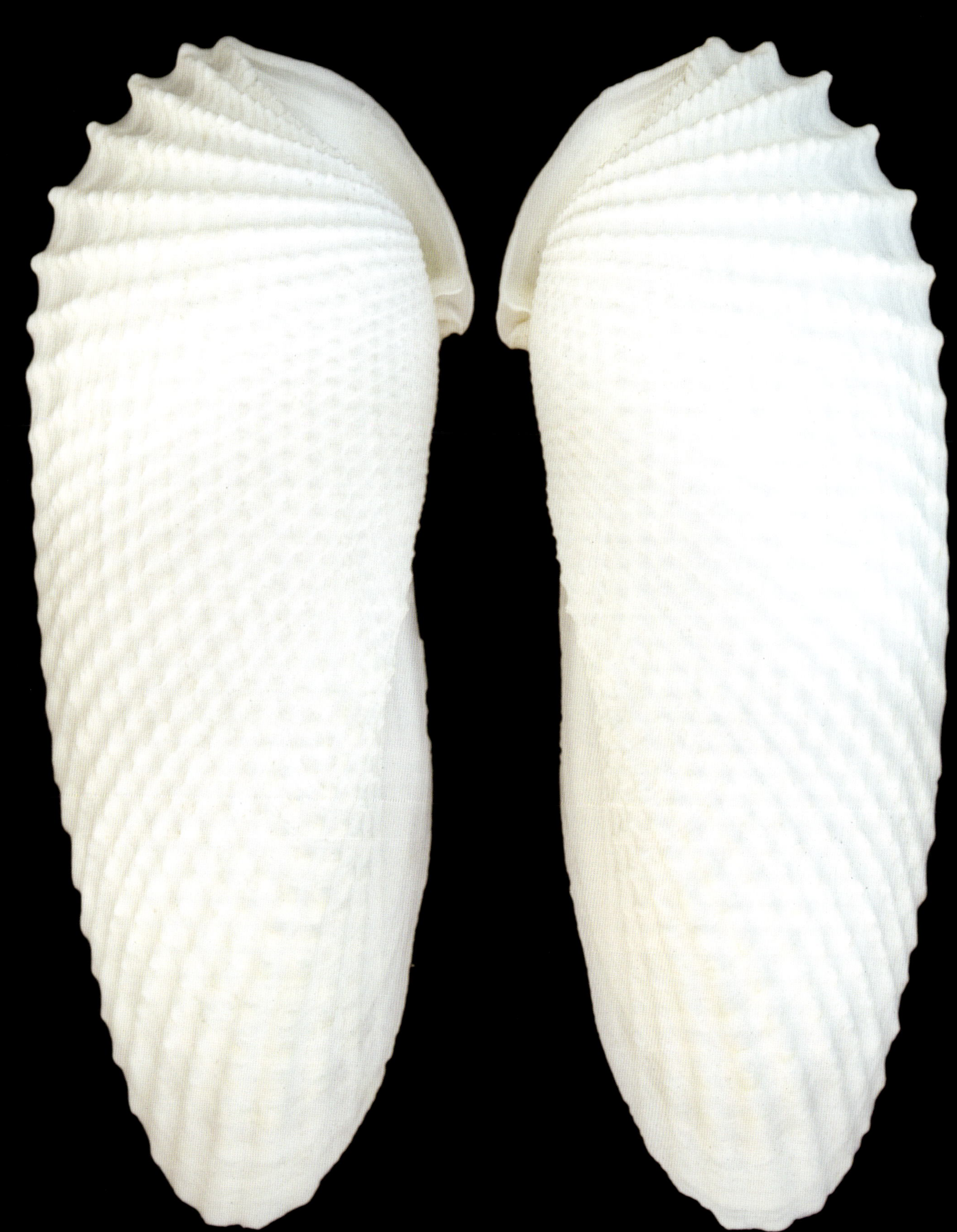

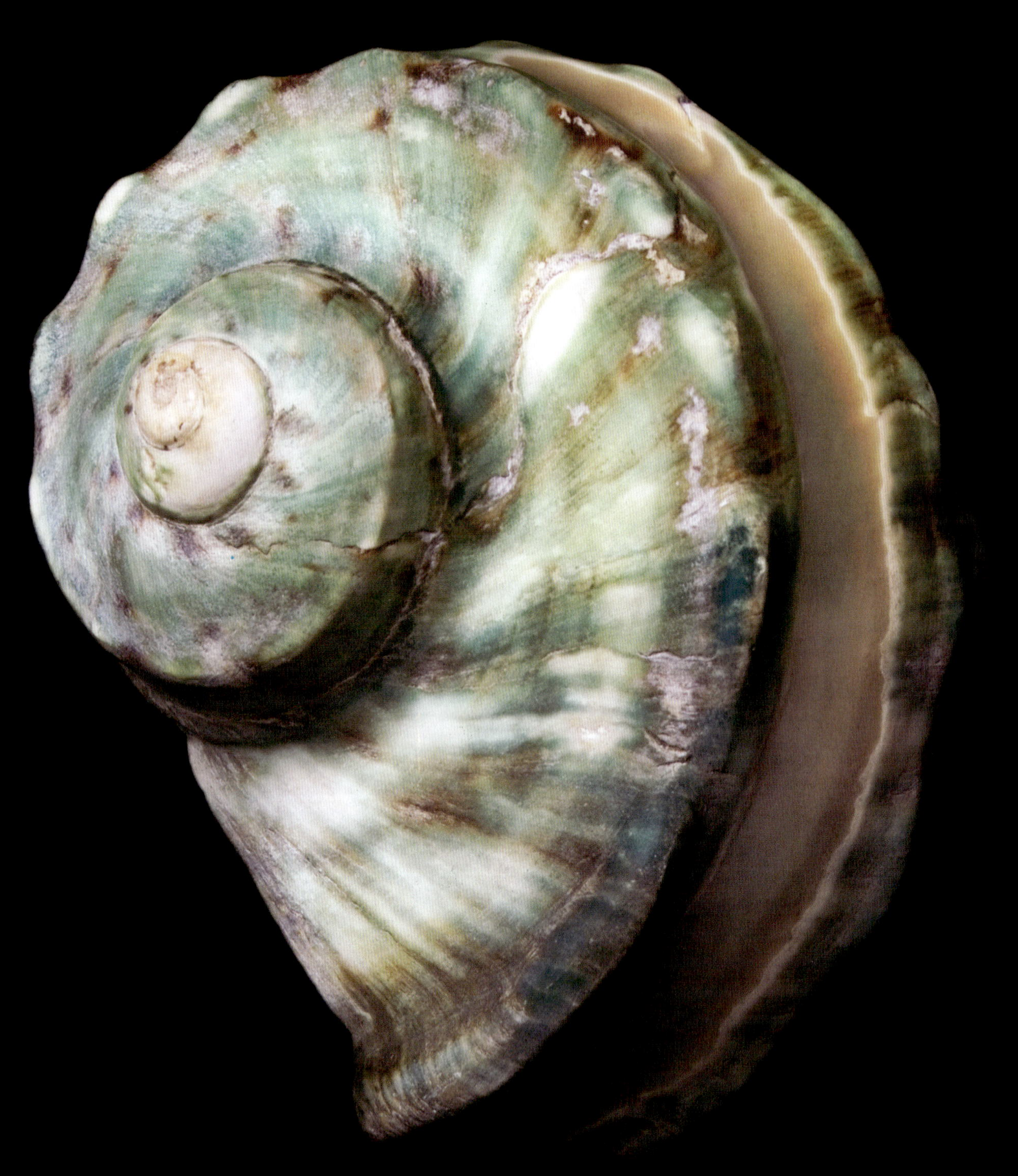

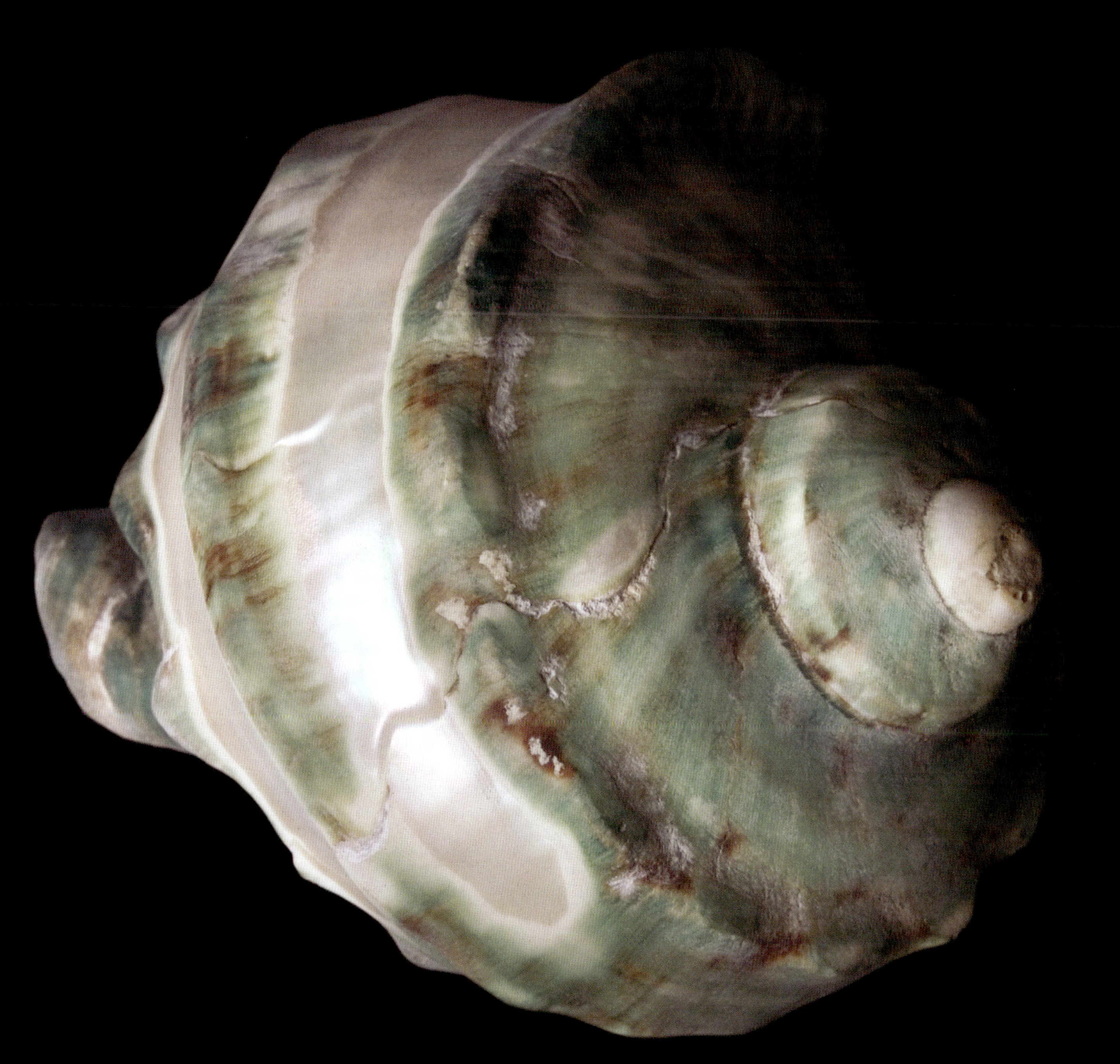

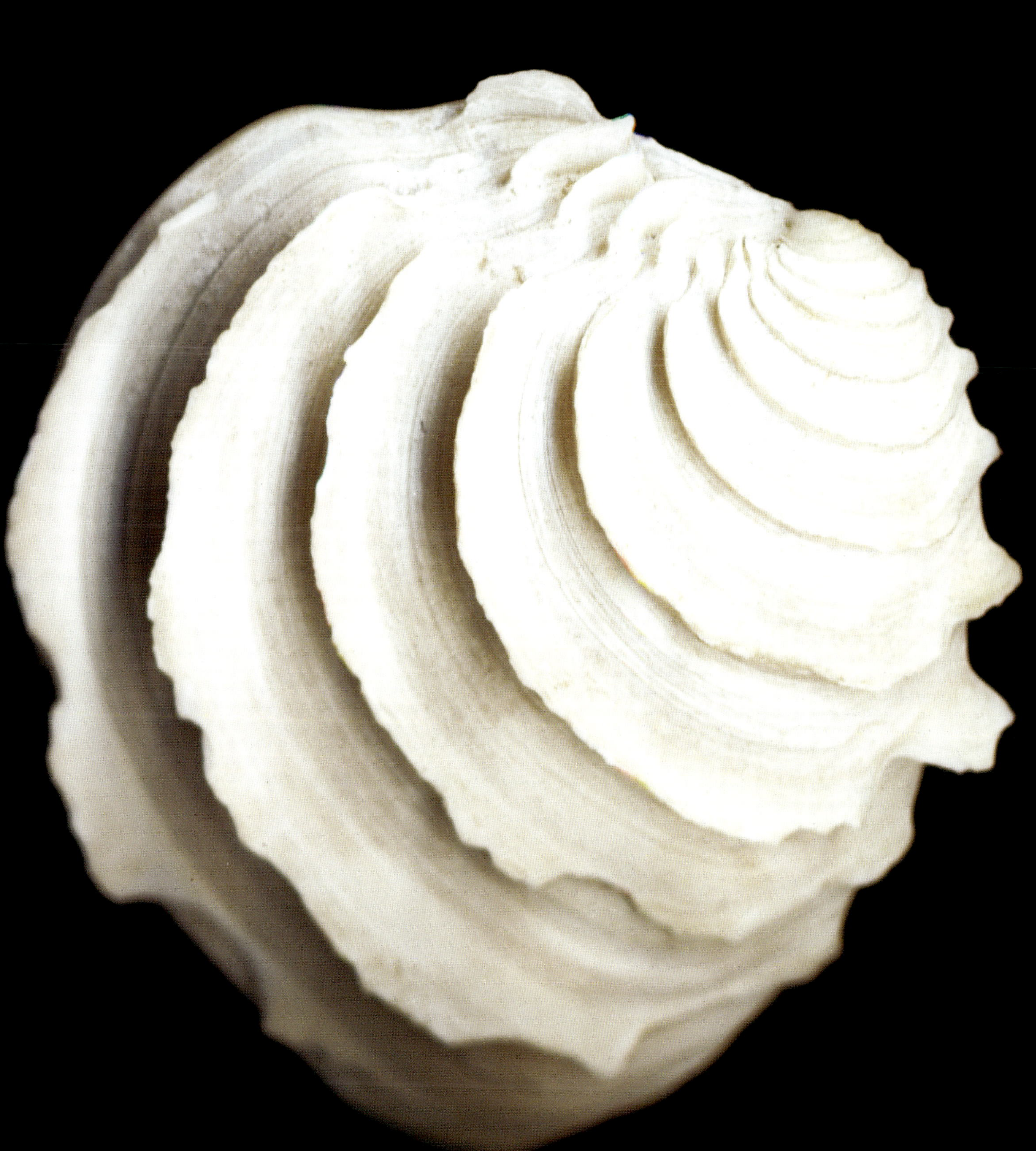

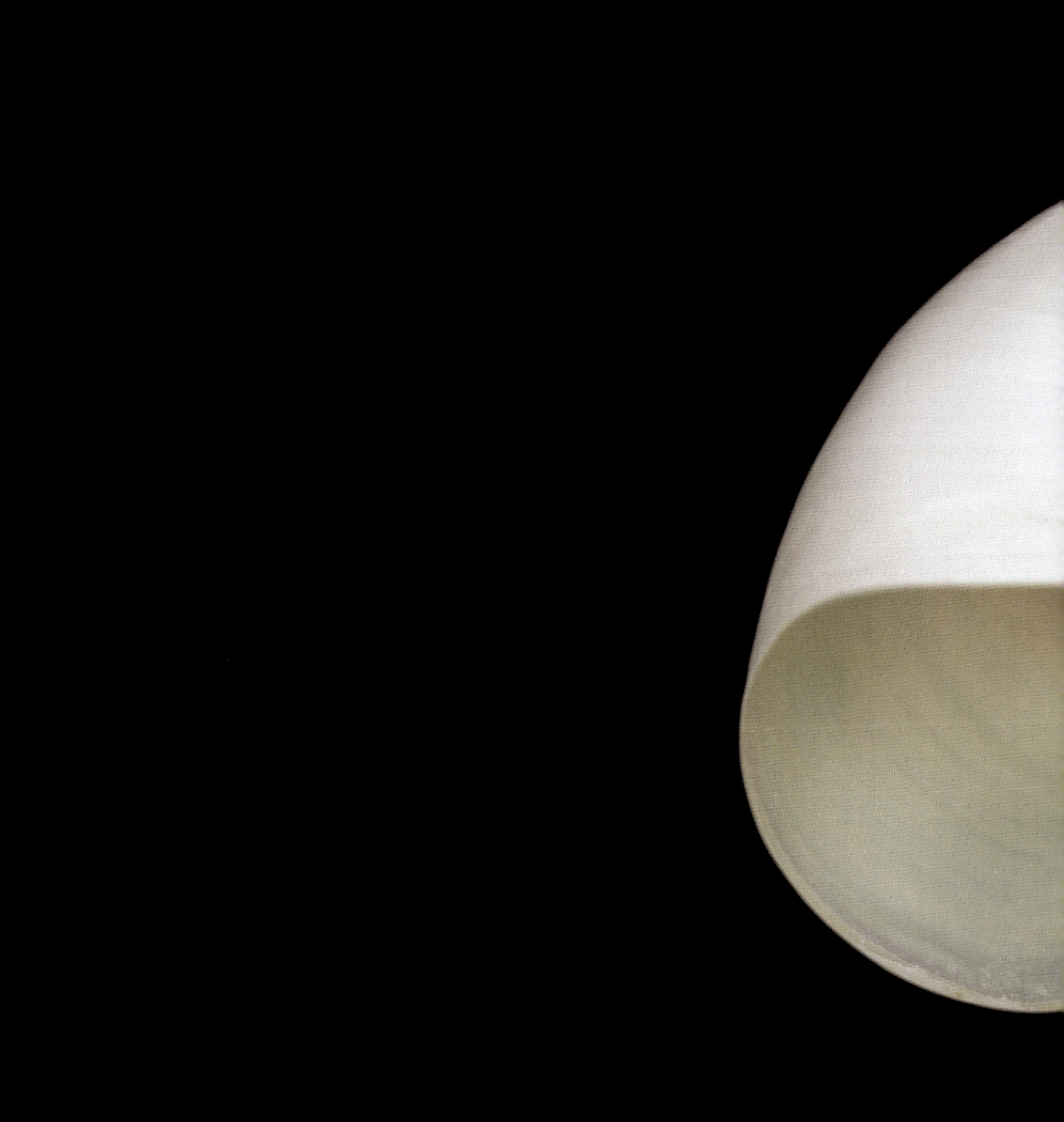

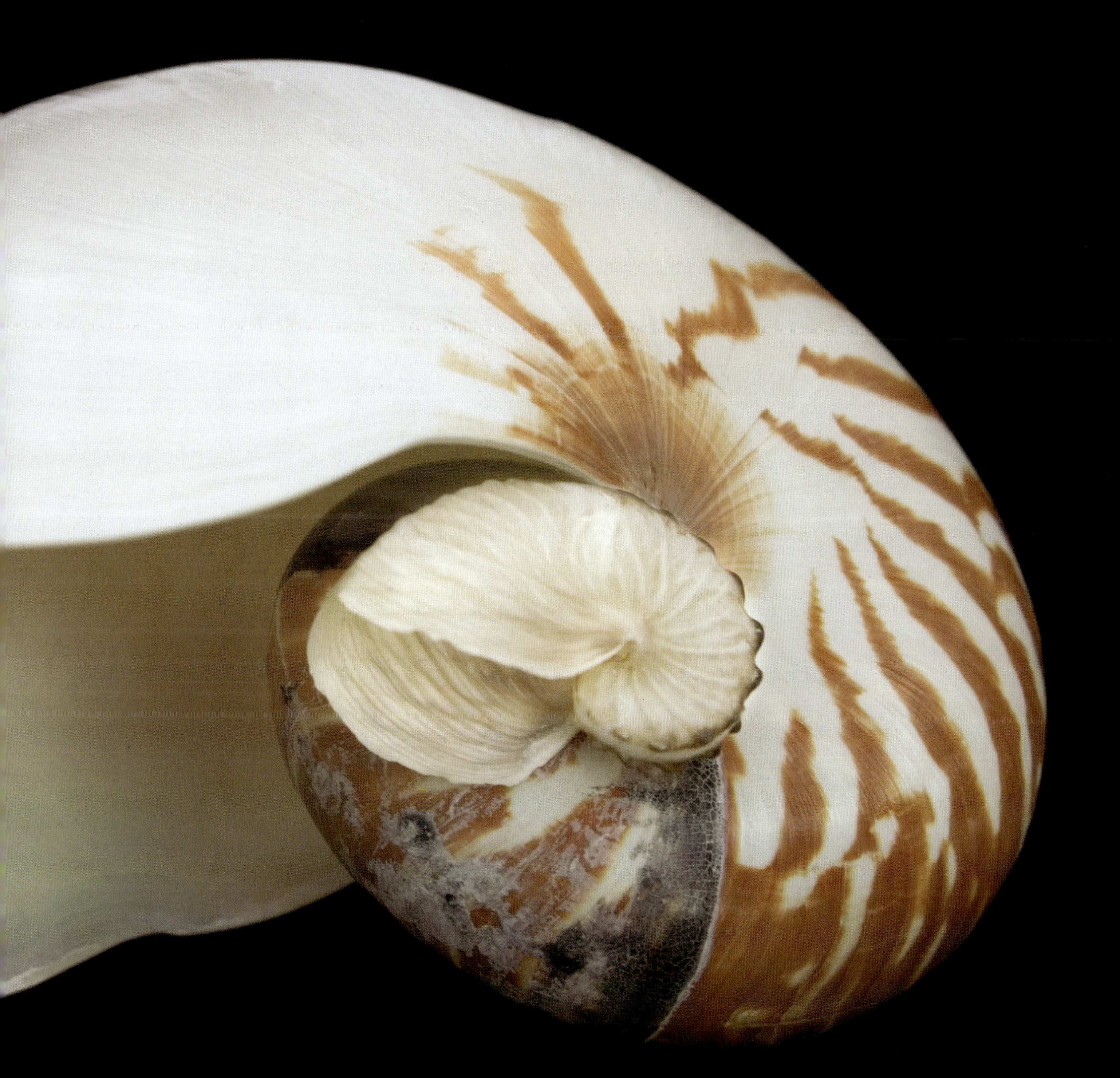

The waves bring back even things we haven't lost.

—Yehuda Amichai

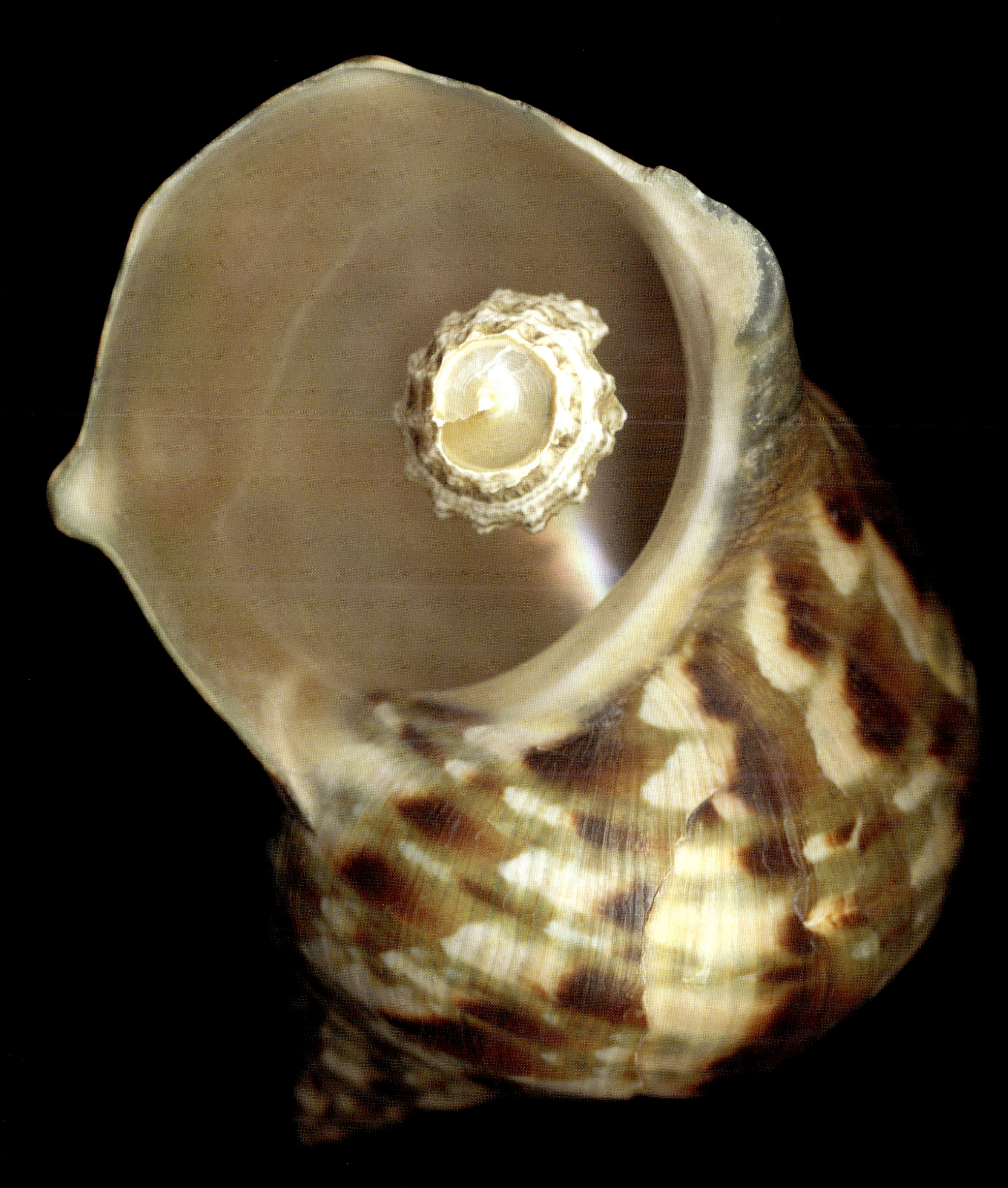

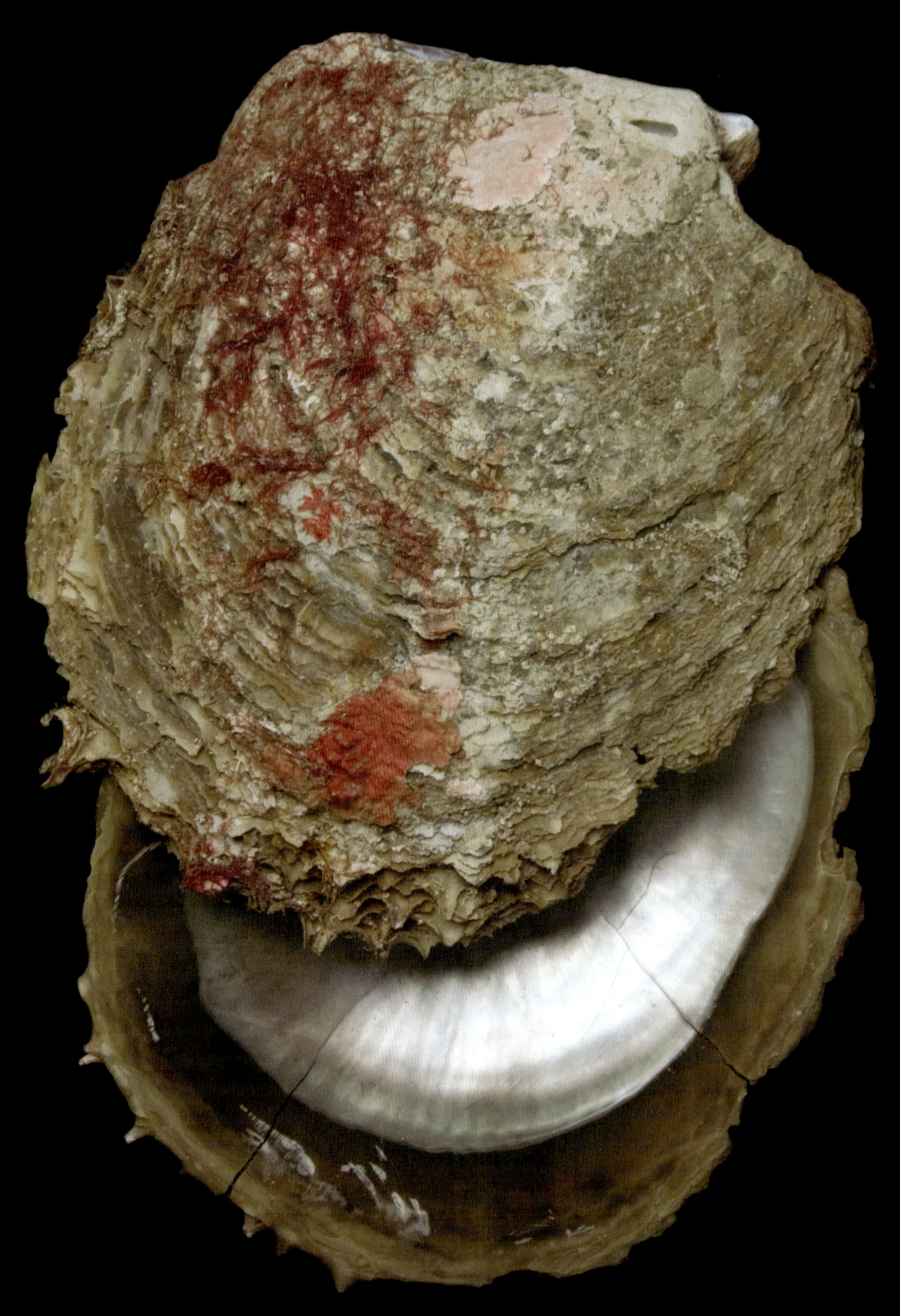

Still I will harvest beauty where it grows.

—Edna St. Vincent Millay

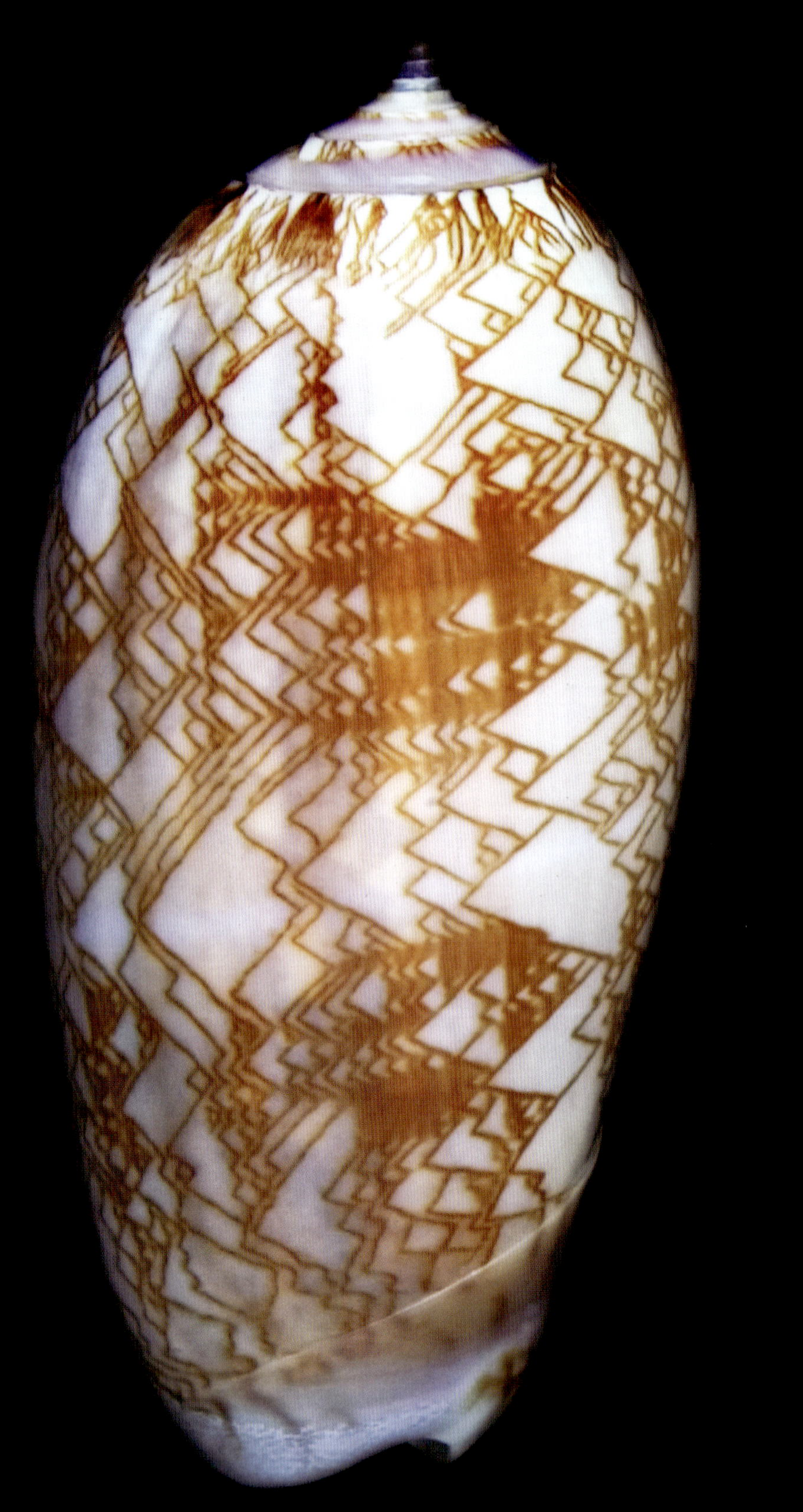

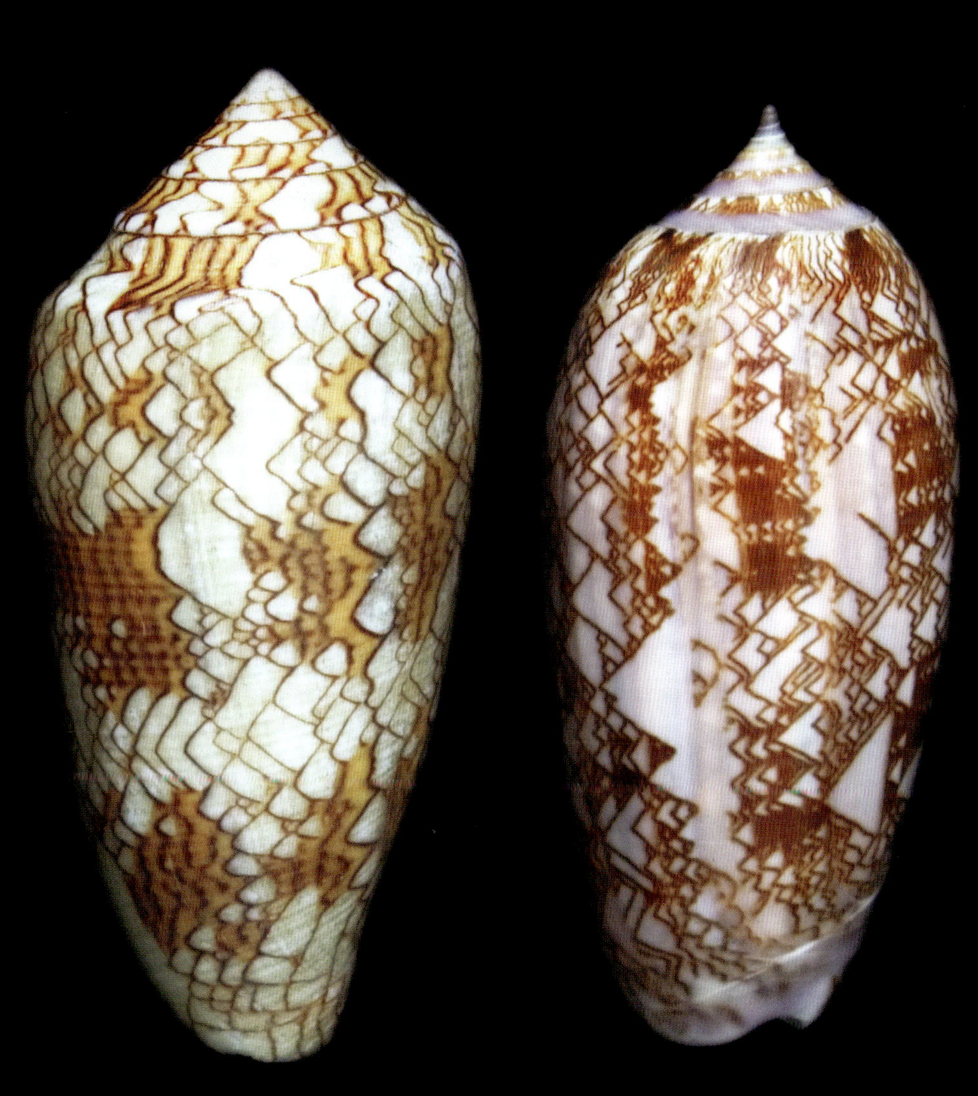

Adopt the pace of nature: her secret is patience.

—Ralph Waldo Emerson

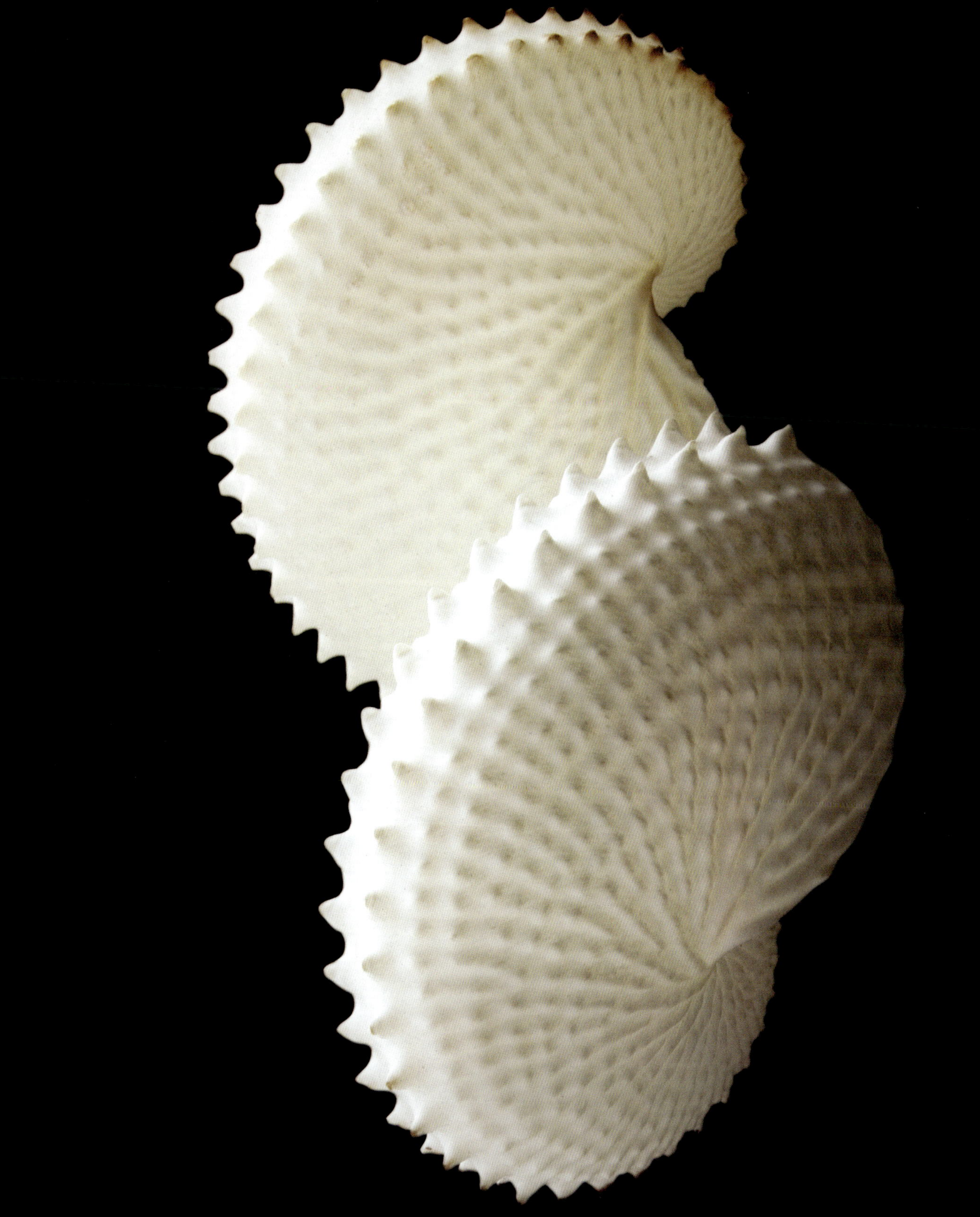

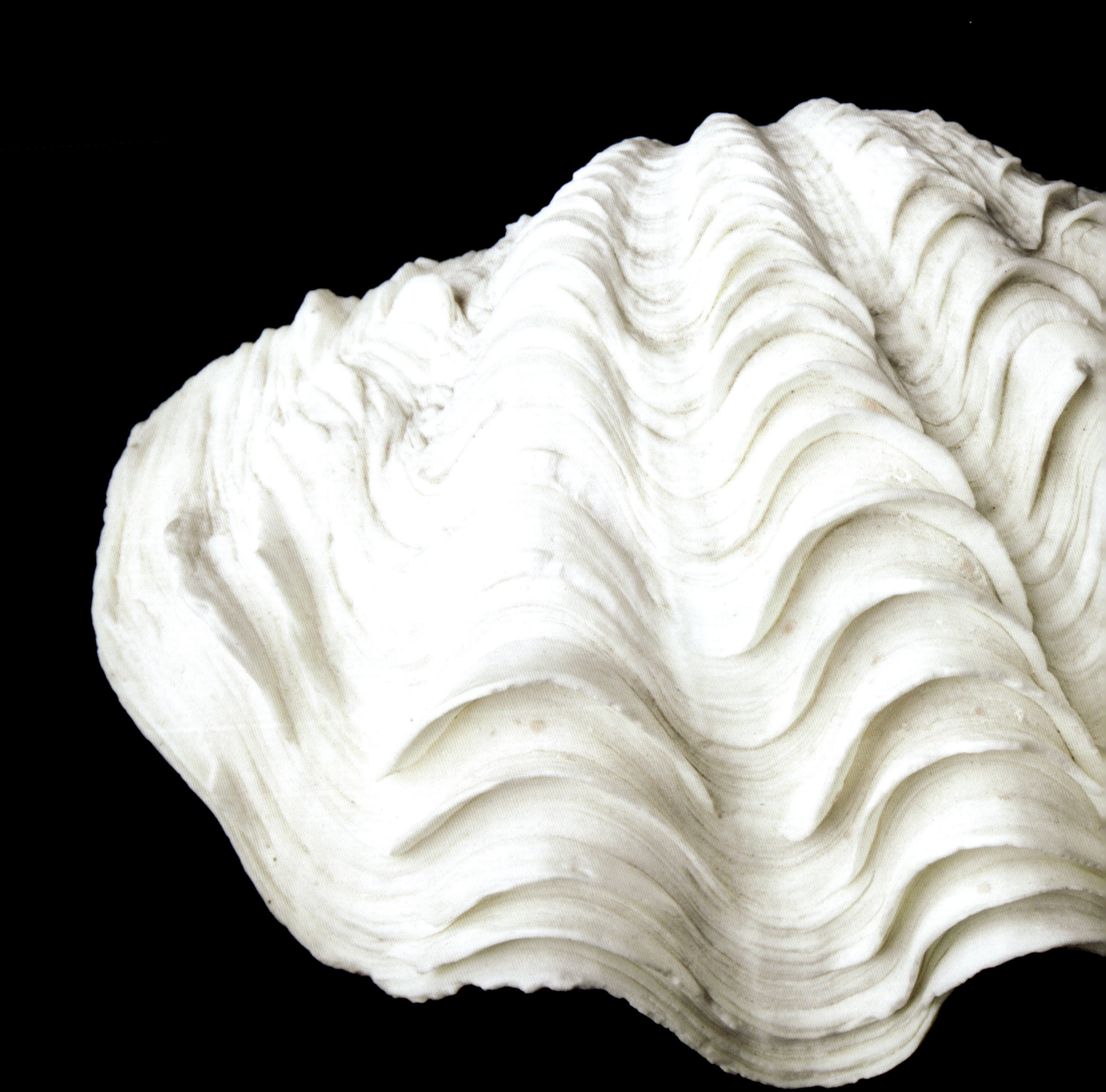

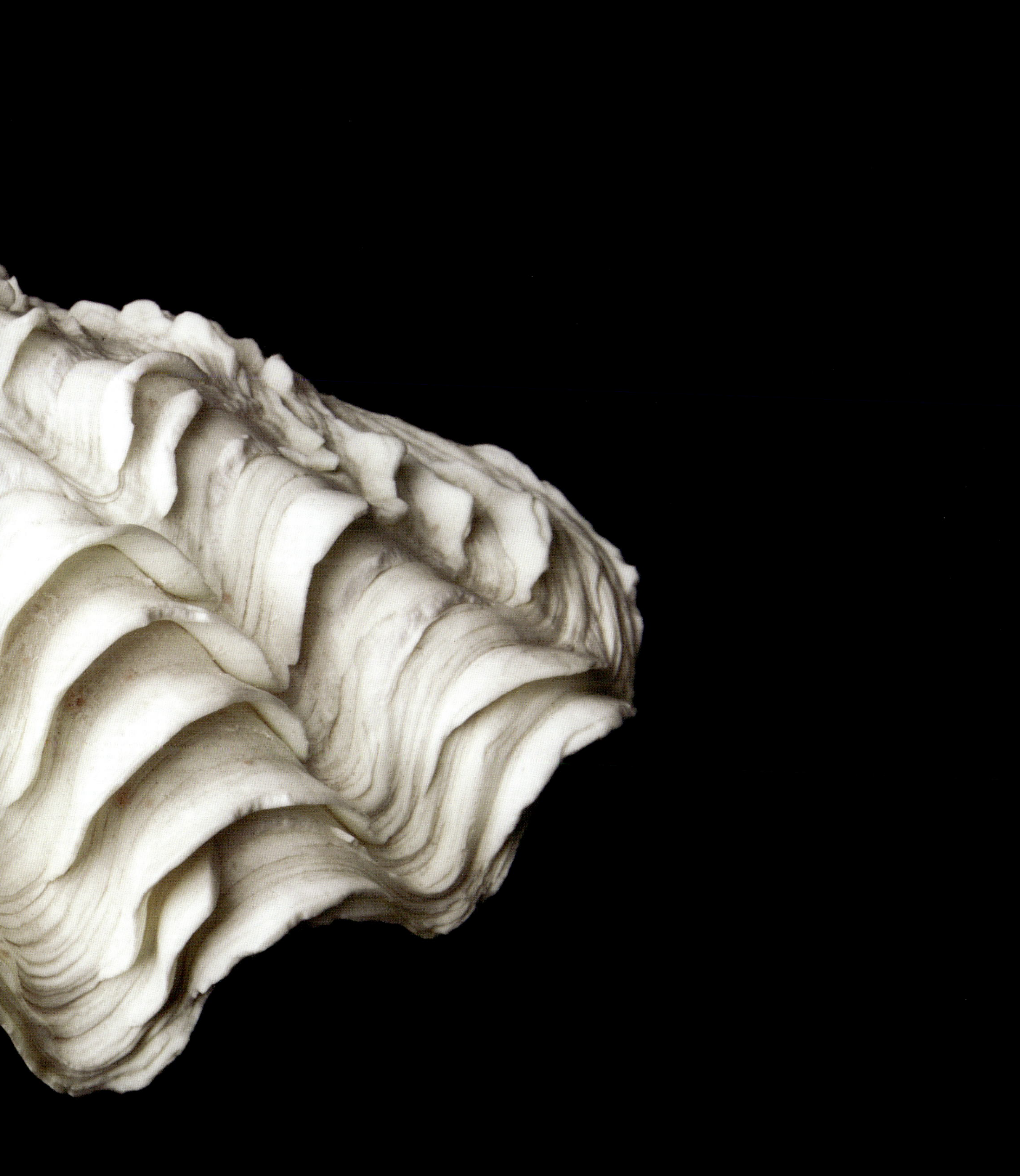

Those who dwell among the beauties and mysteries of the earth are never alone or weary of life.

—Rachel Carson

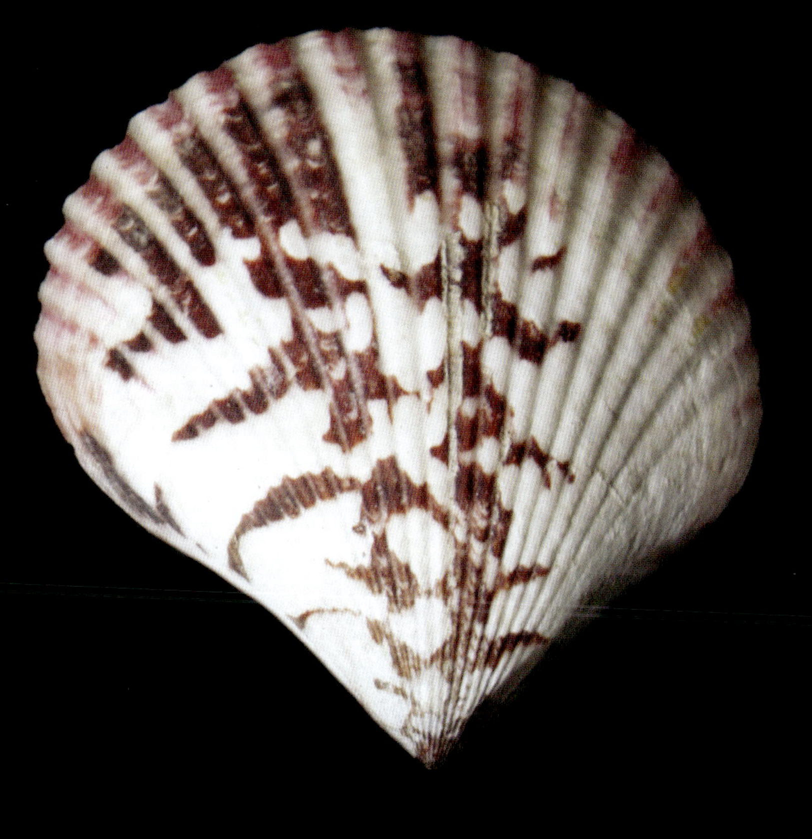

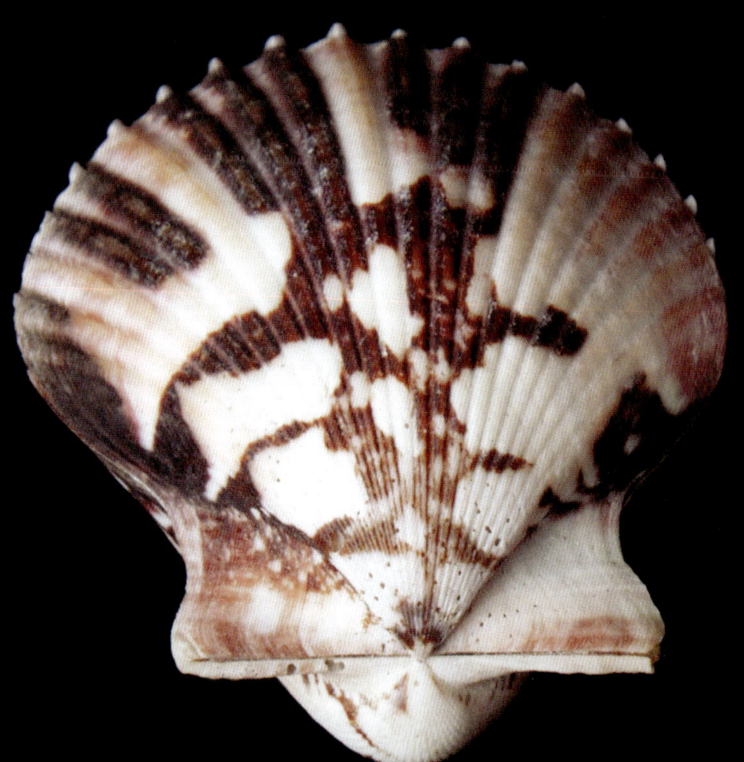

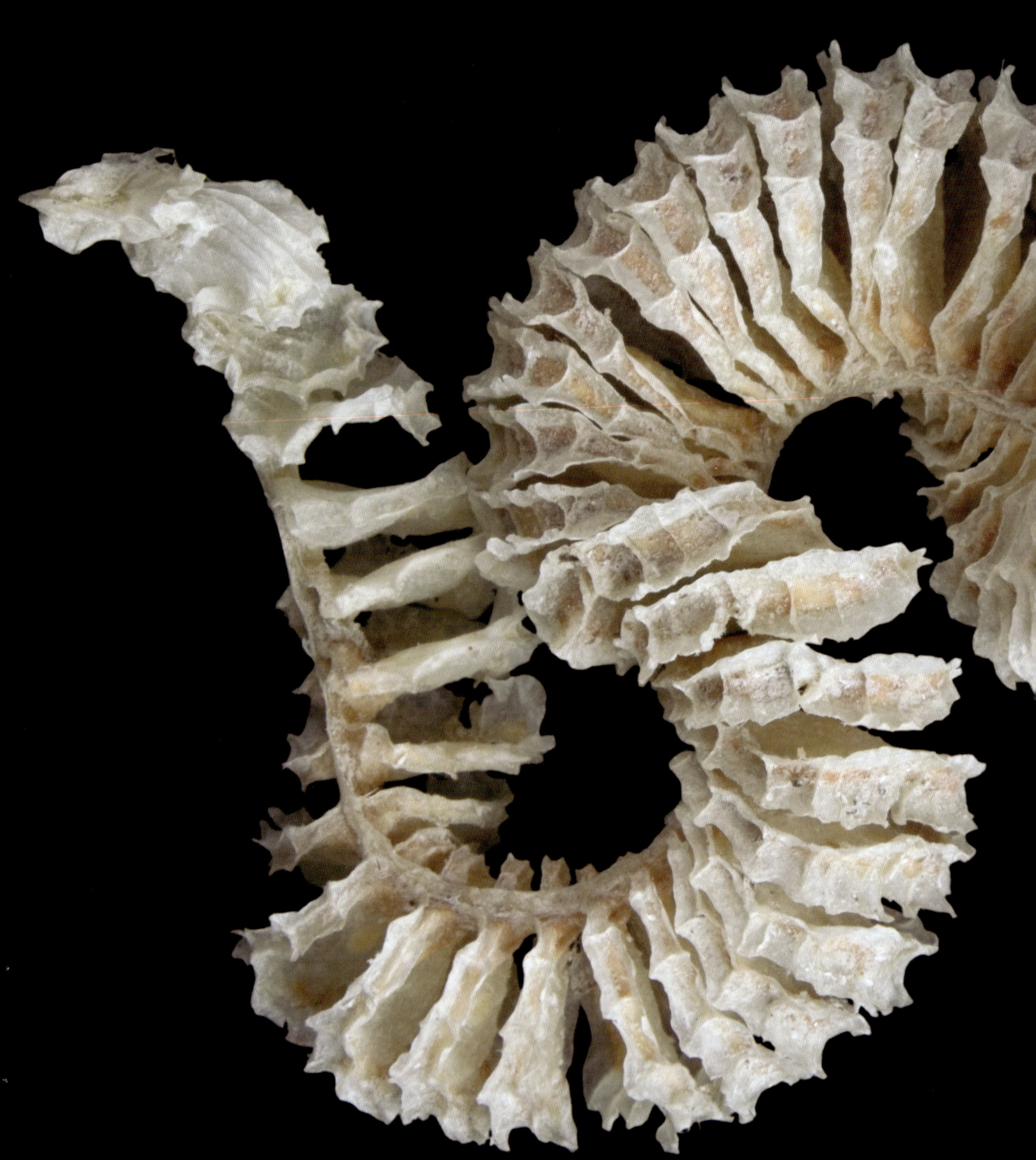

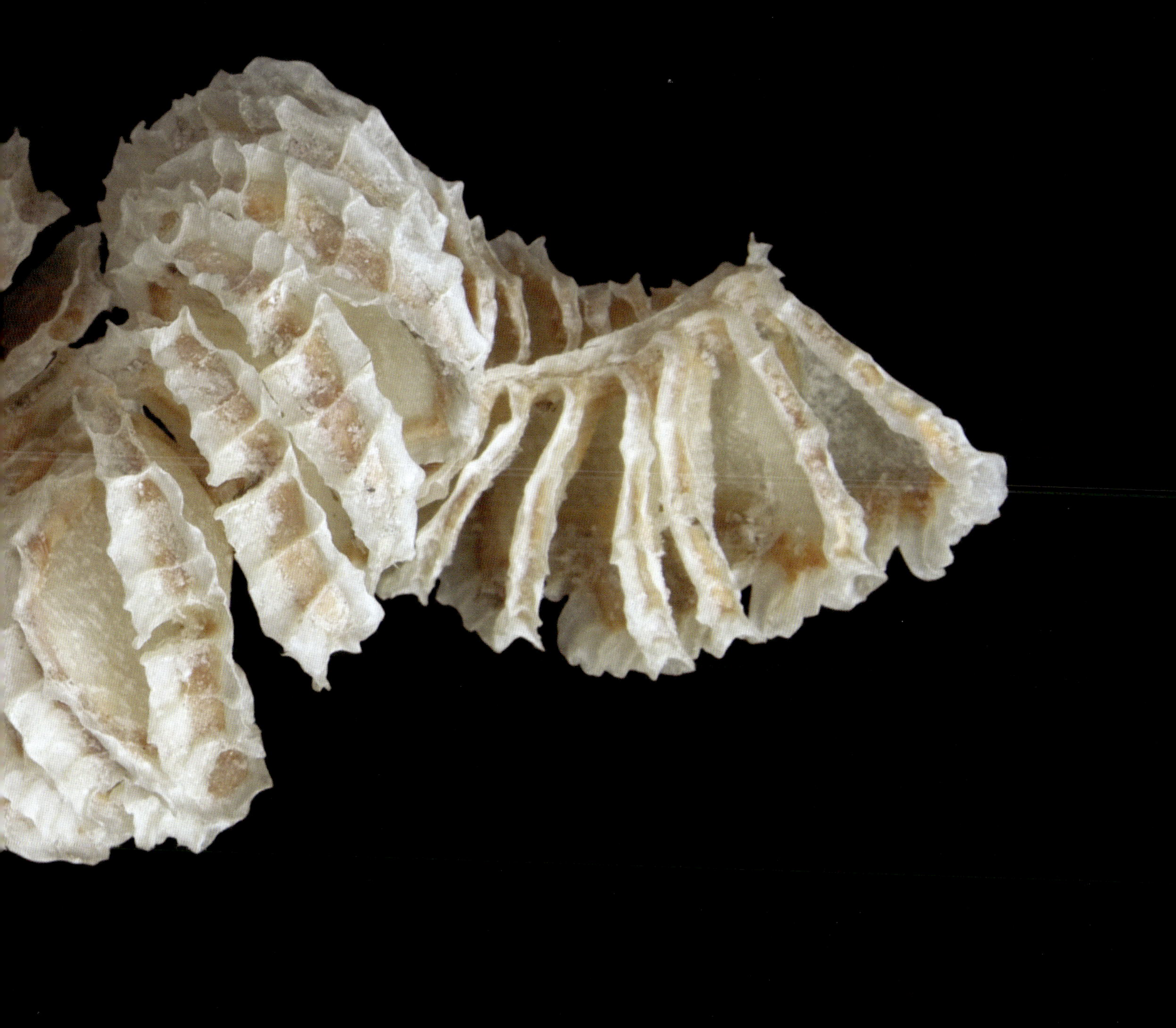

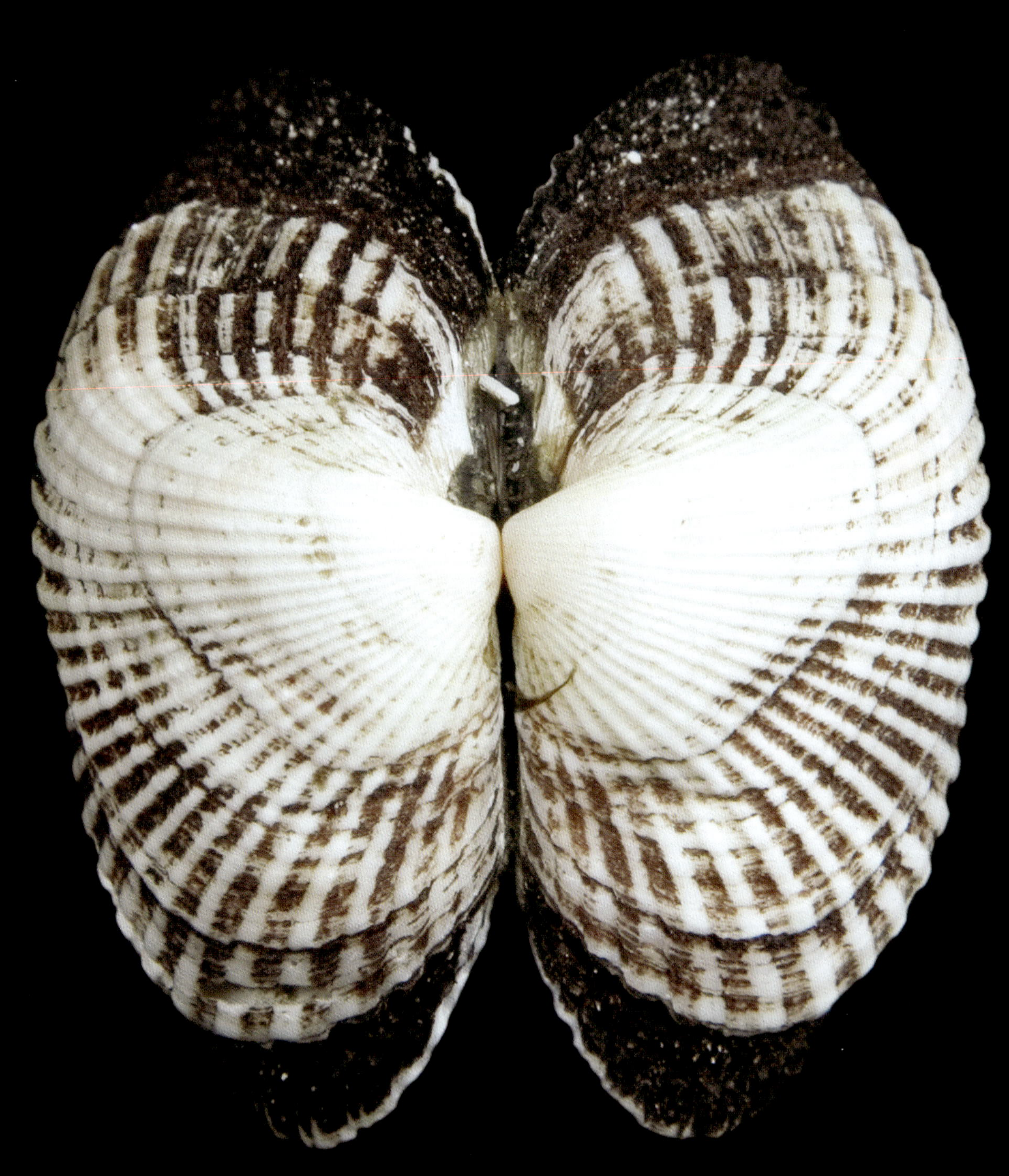

The butterfly counts not months but moments, and has time enough.

—Rabindranath Tagore

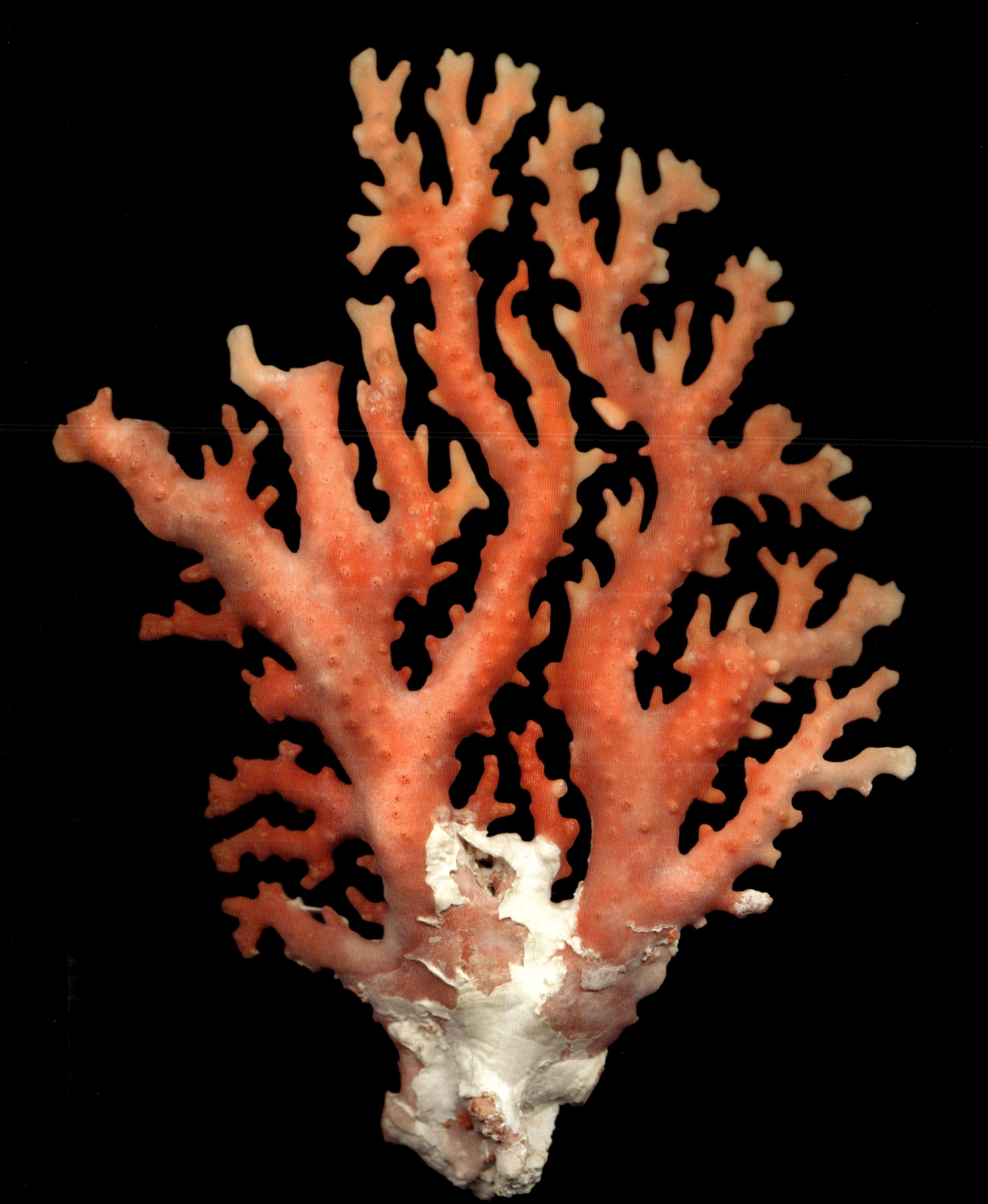

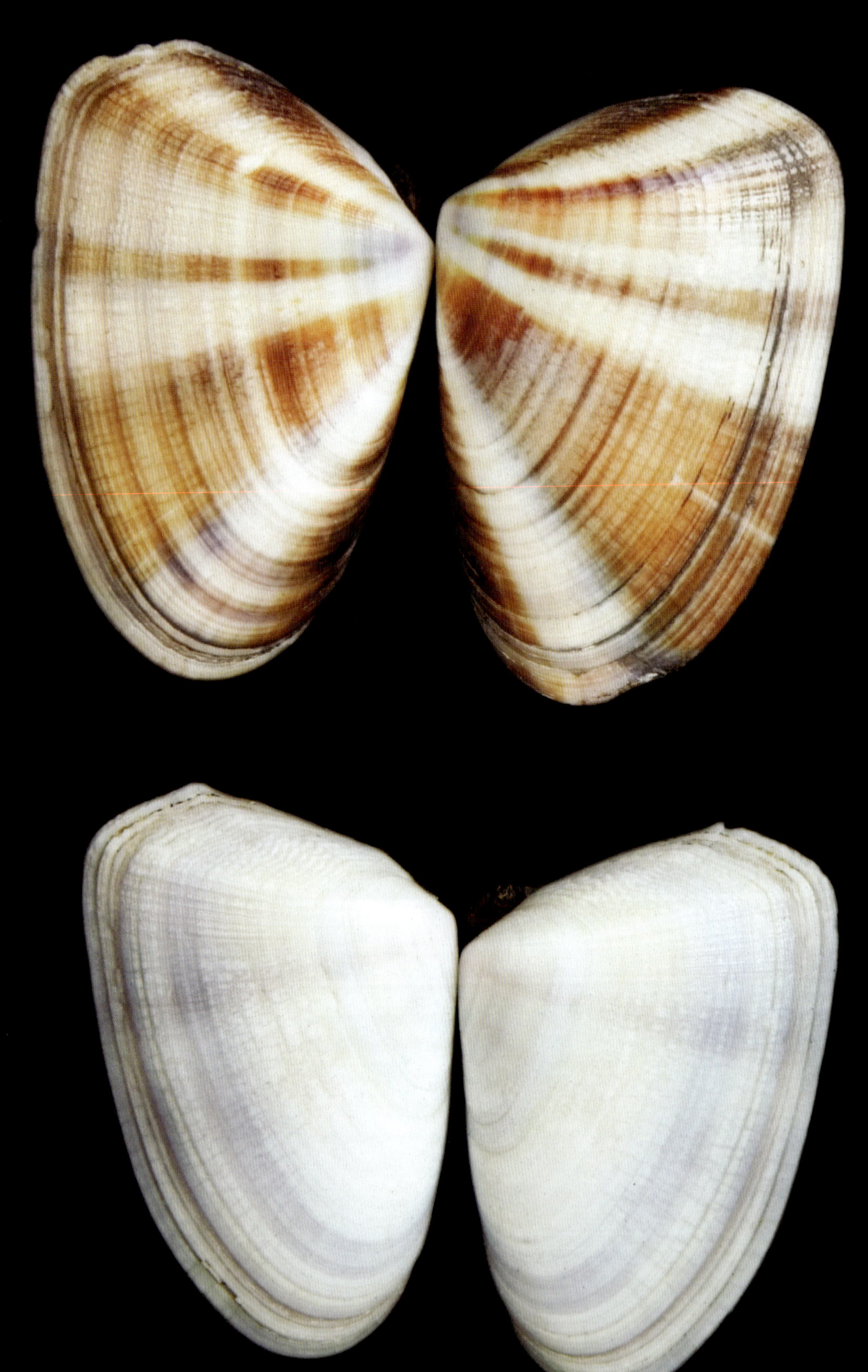

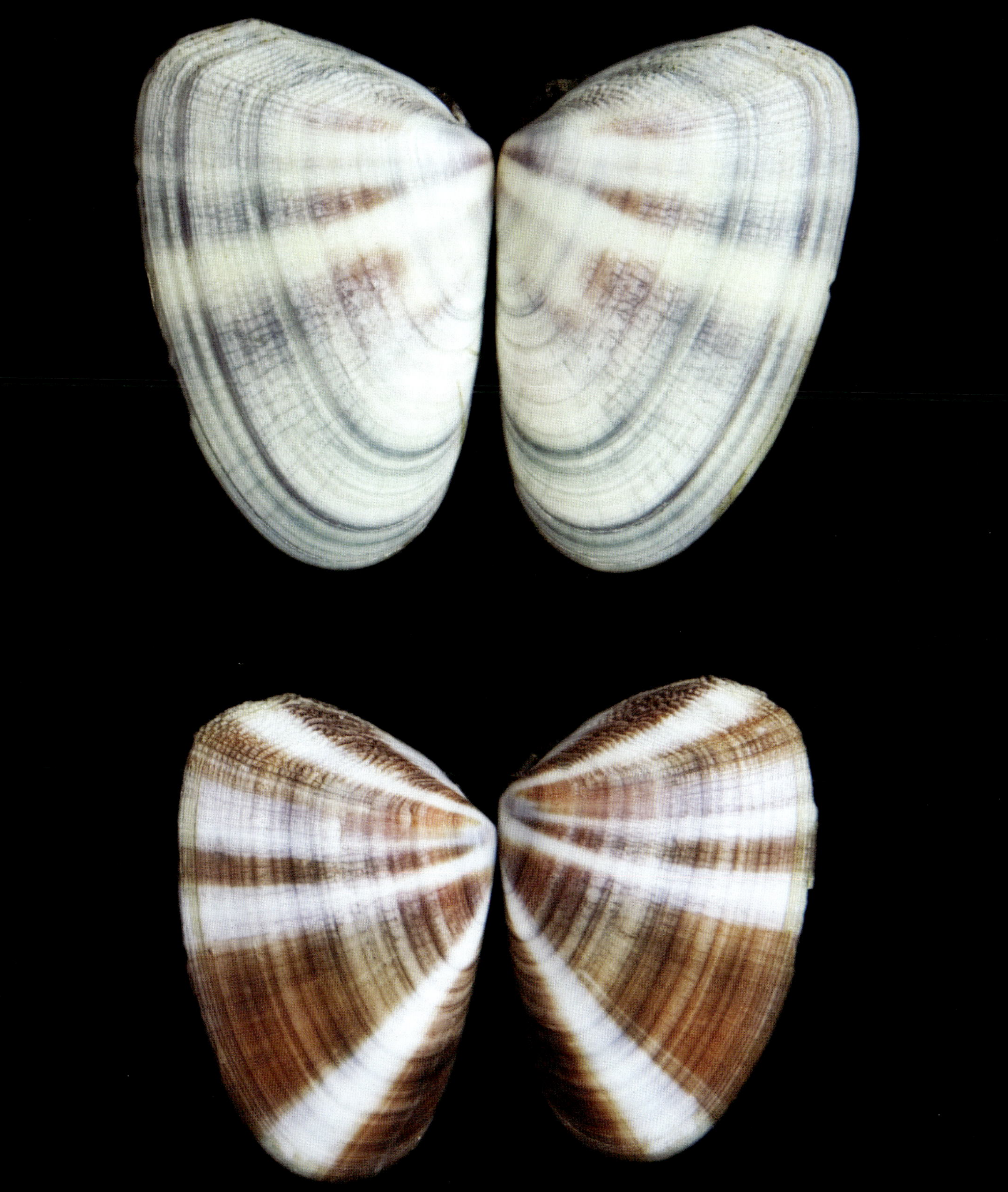

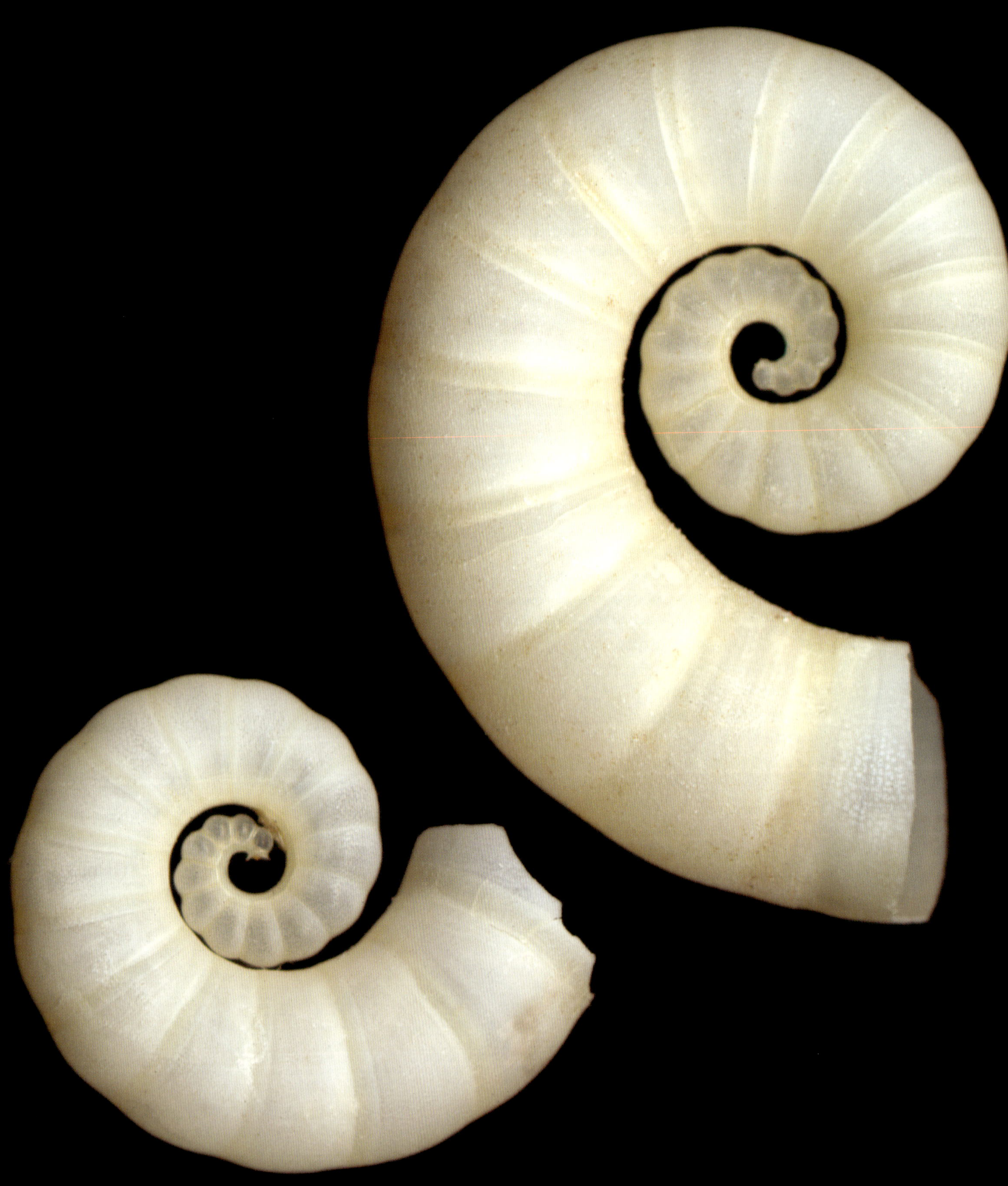

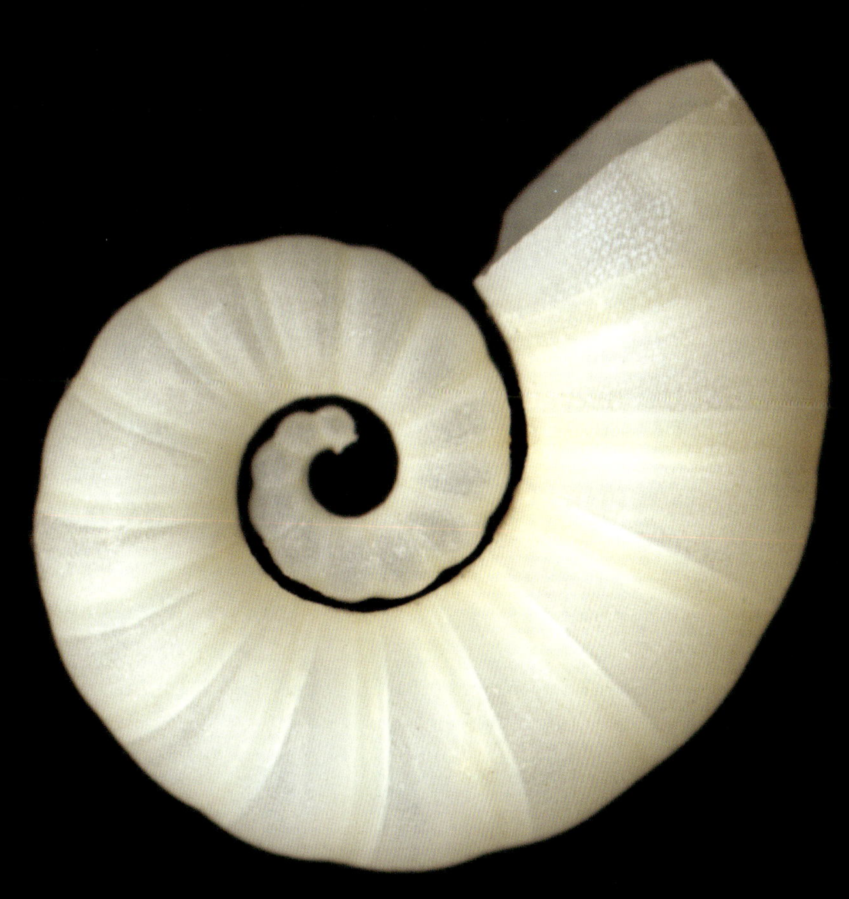

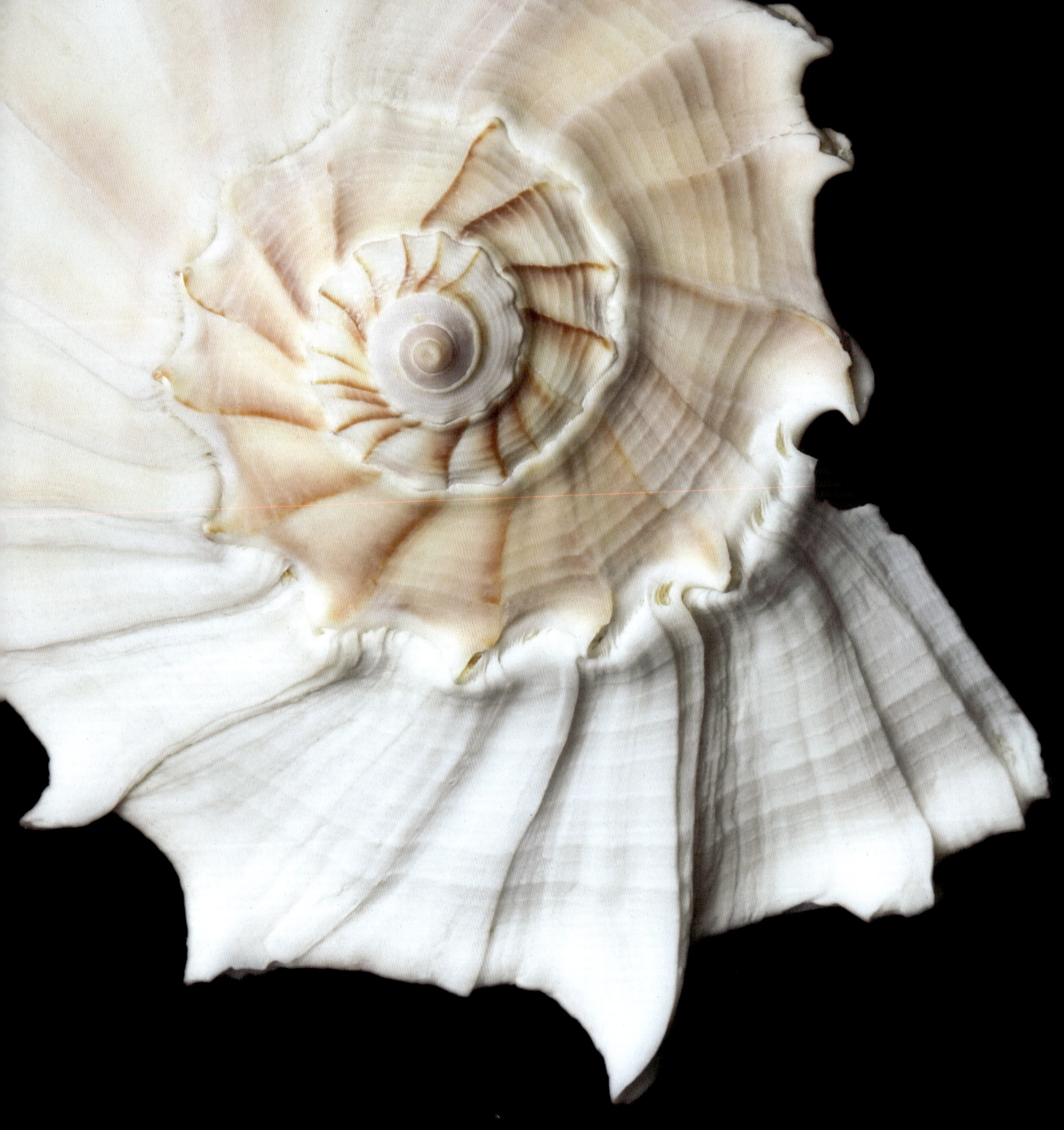

The world offers itself to your imagination.

—Mary Oliver

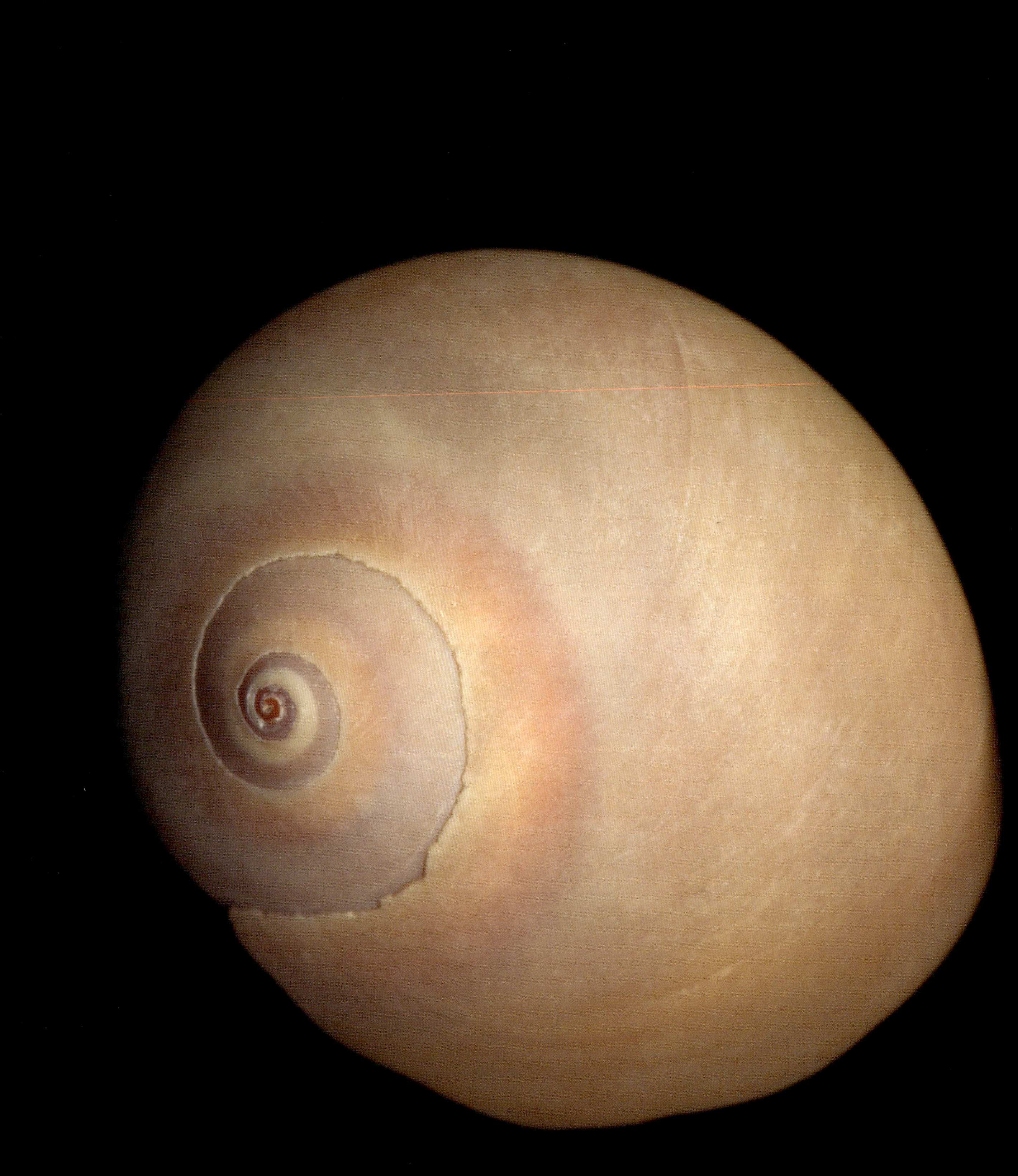

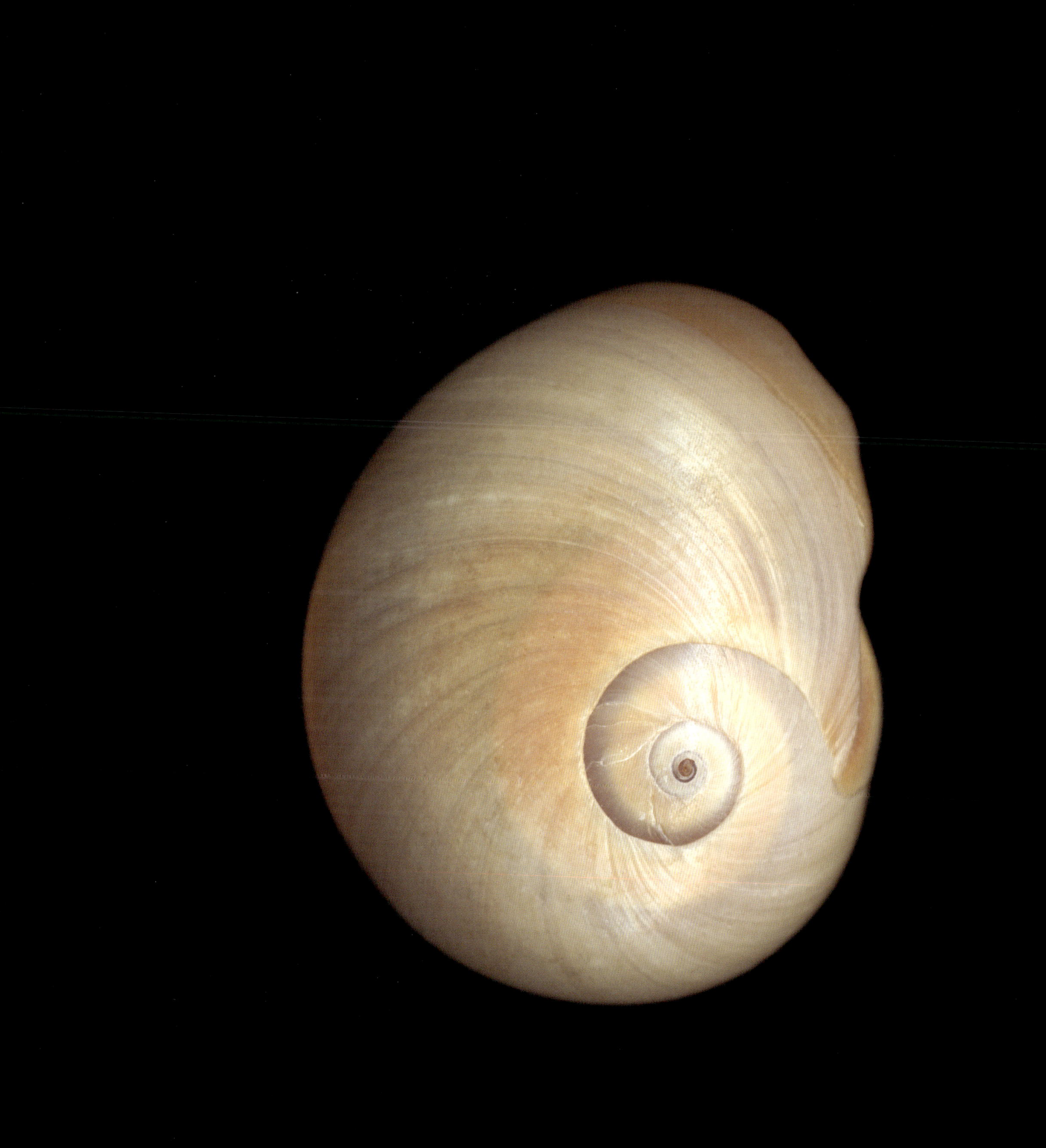

The creation of a thousand forests is in one acorn.

—Ralph Waldo Emerson

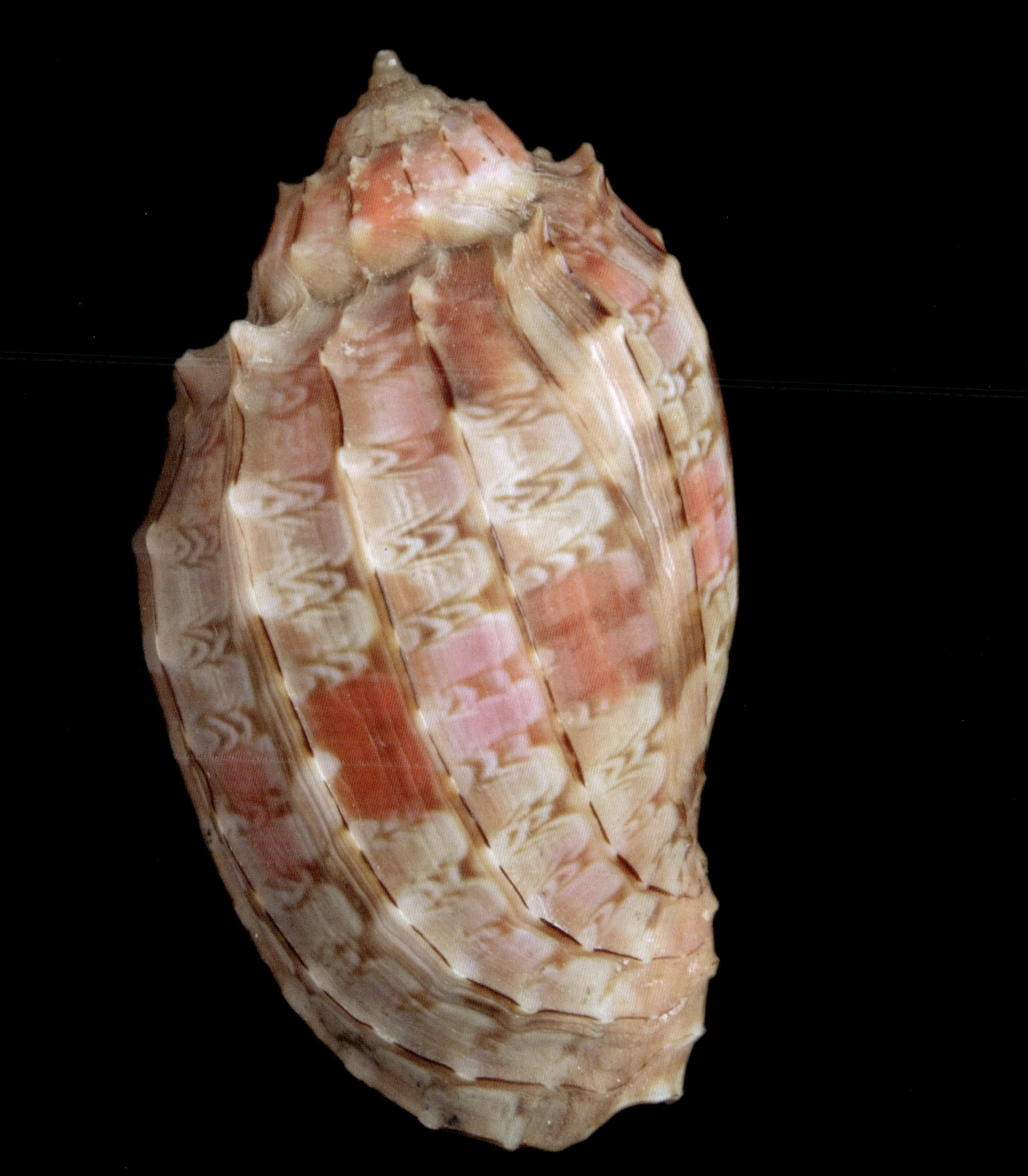

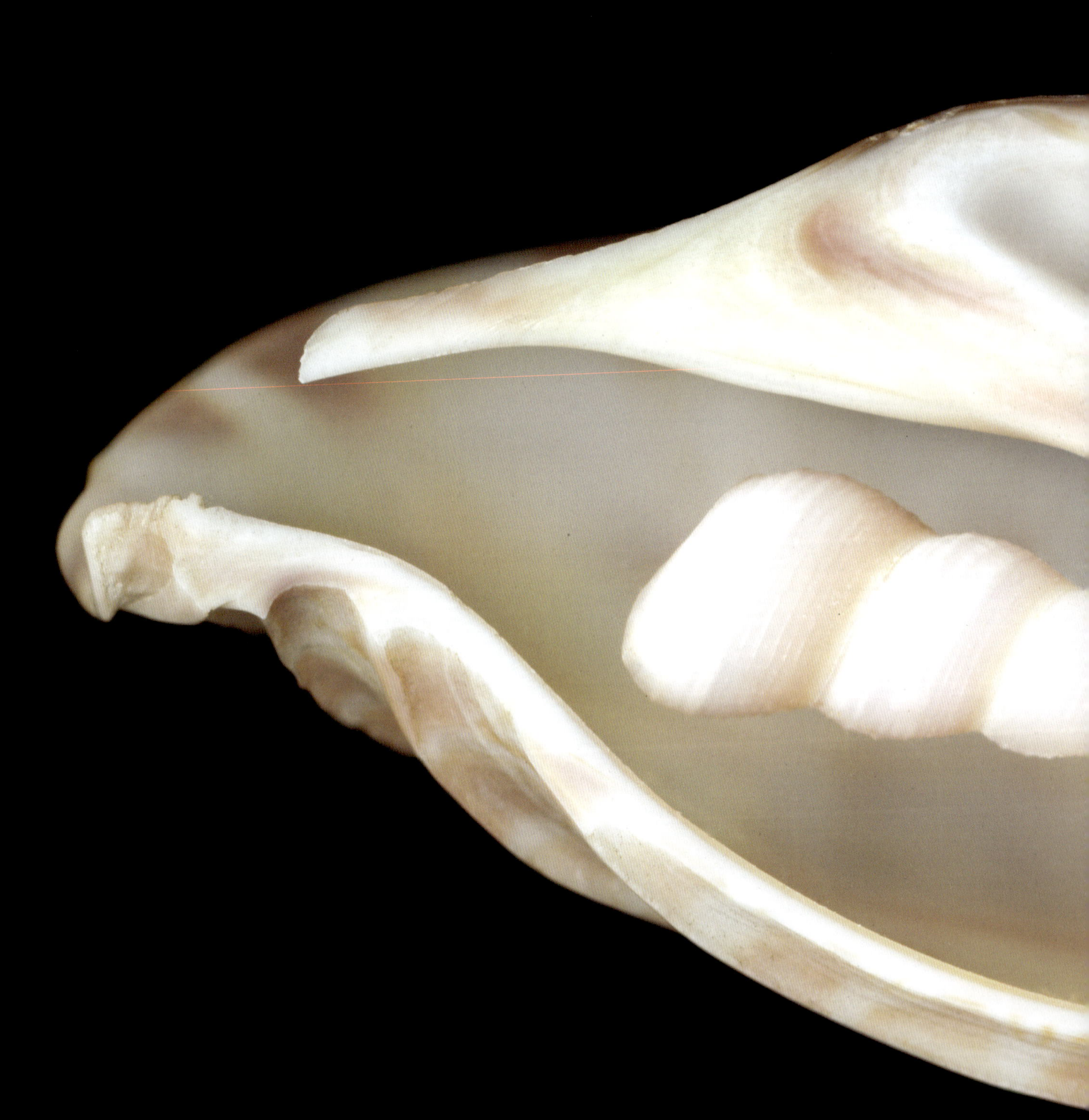

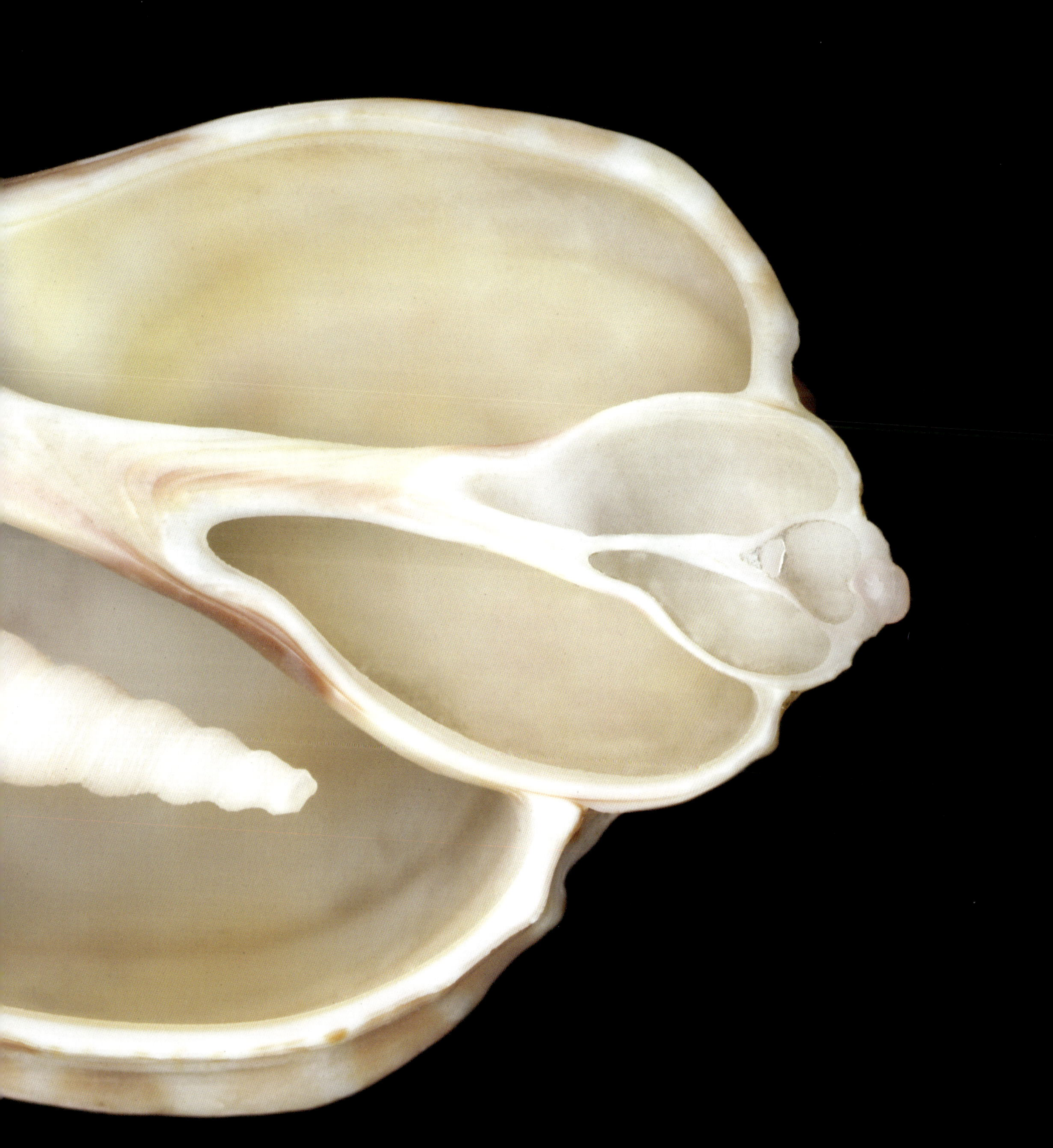

Nature always wears the colors of the spirit.

—Ralph Waldo Emerson

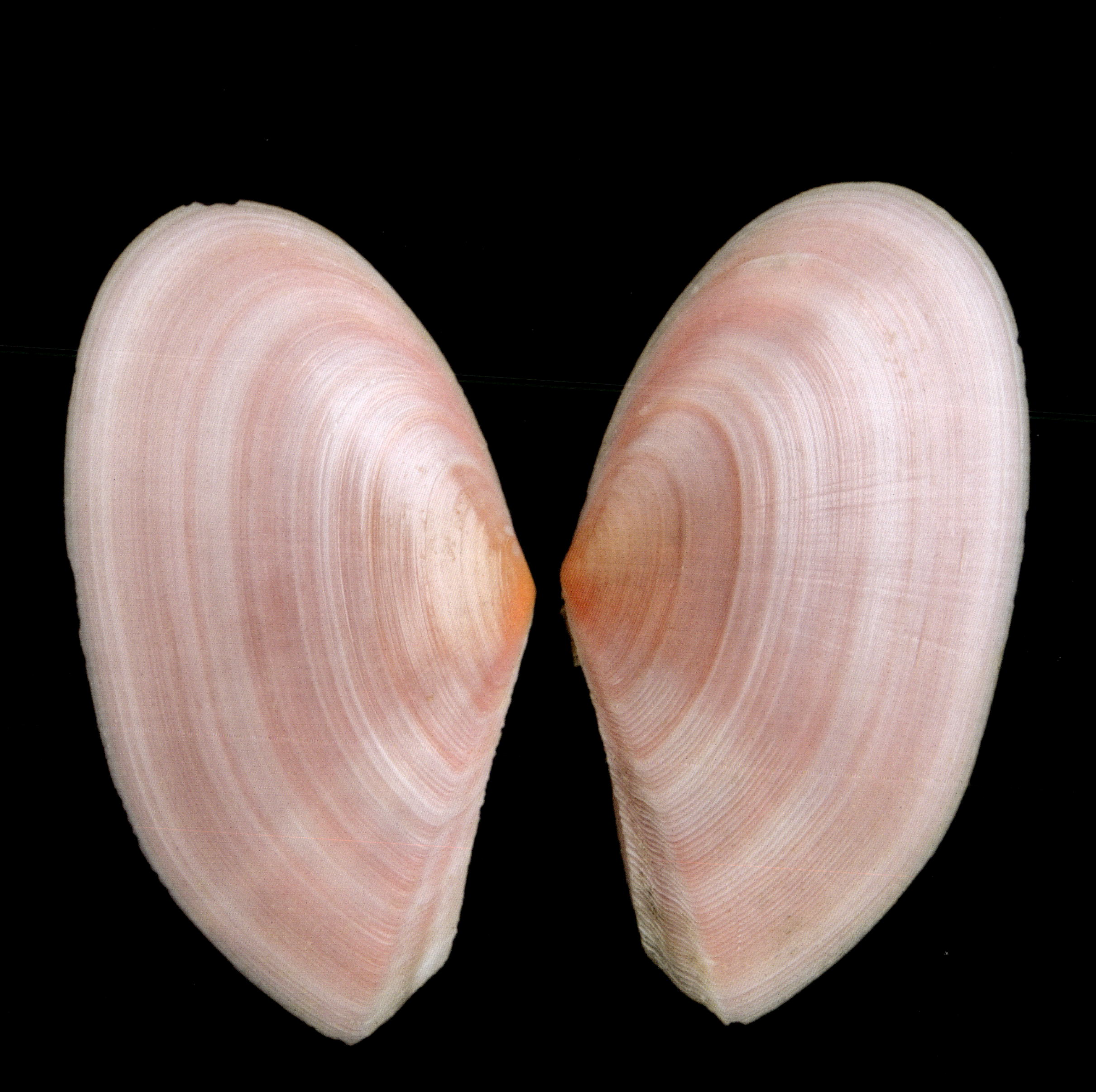

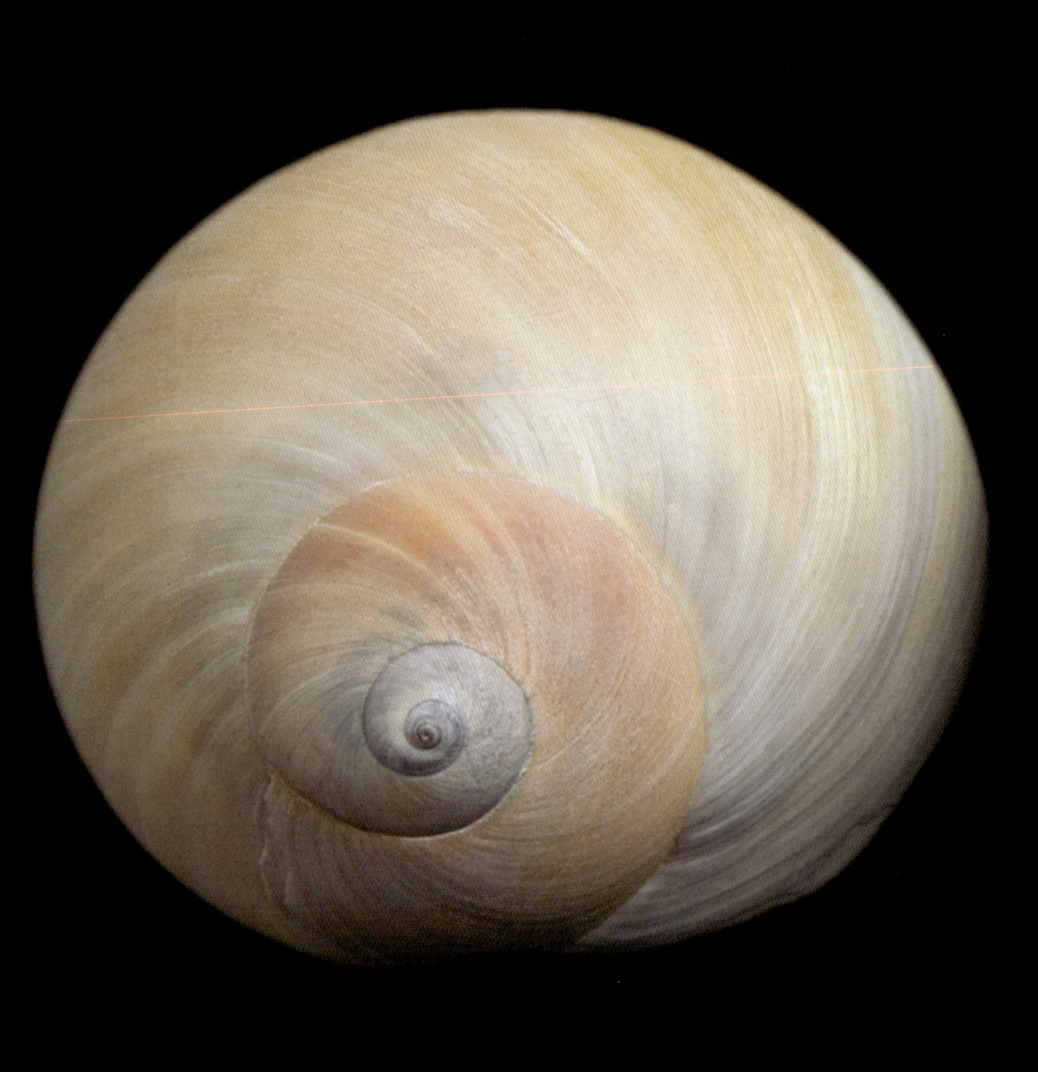

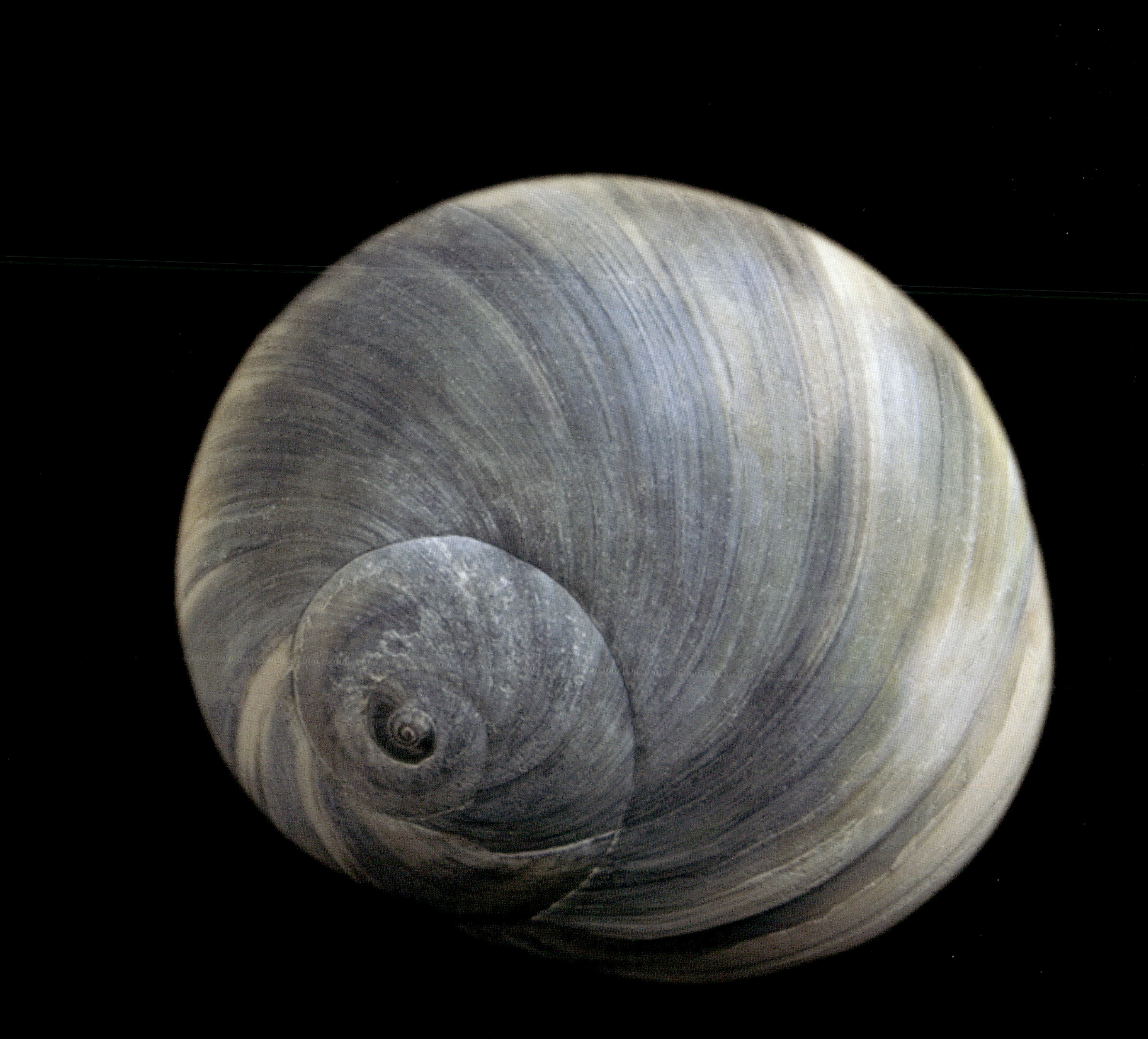

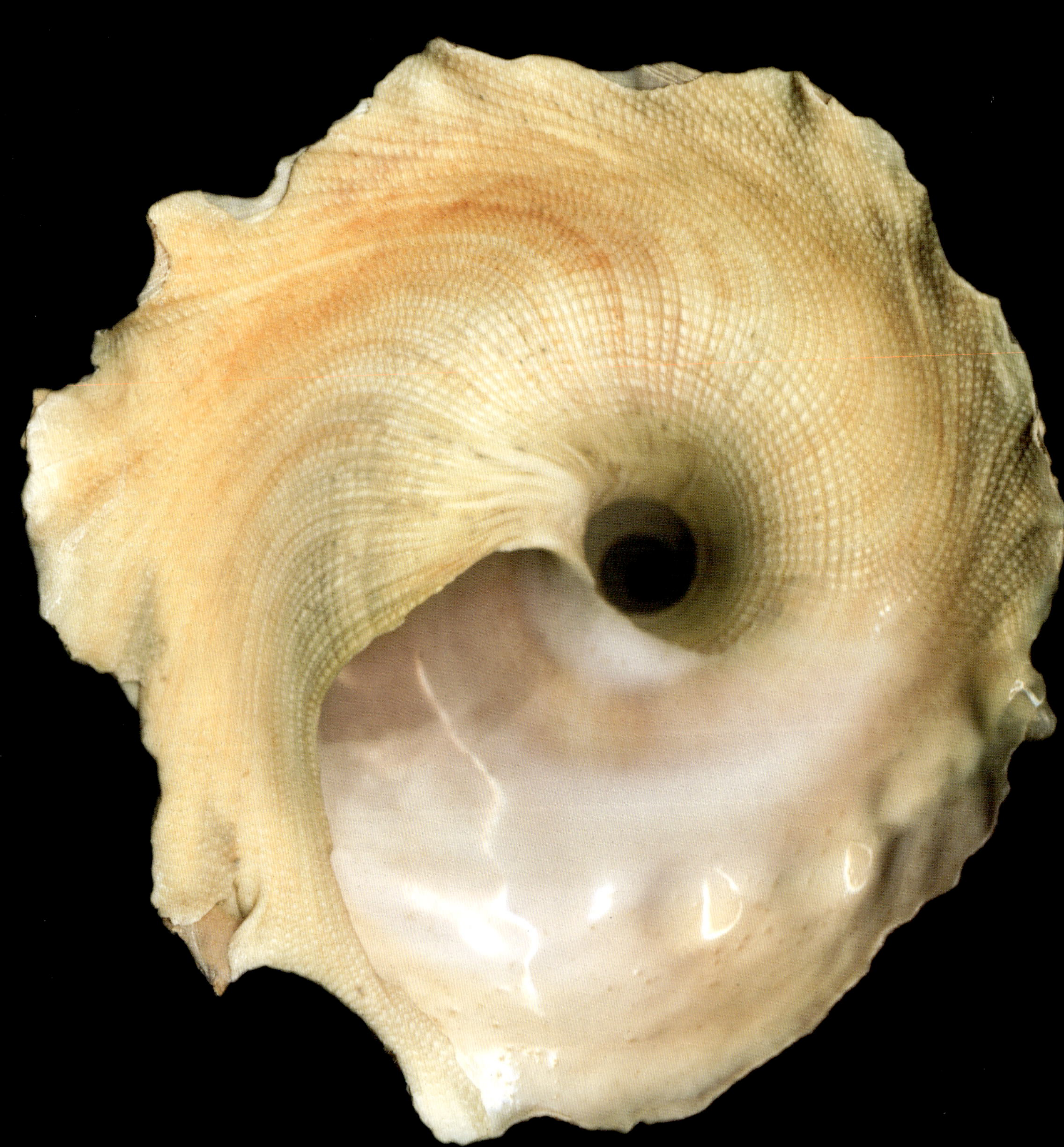

Make no small plans for they have no power to stir the soul.

—Niccolo Machiavelli

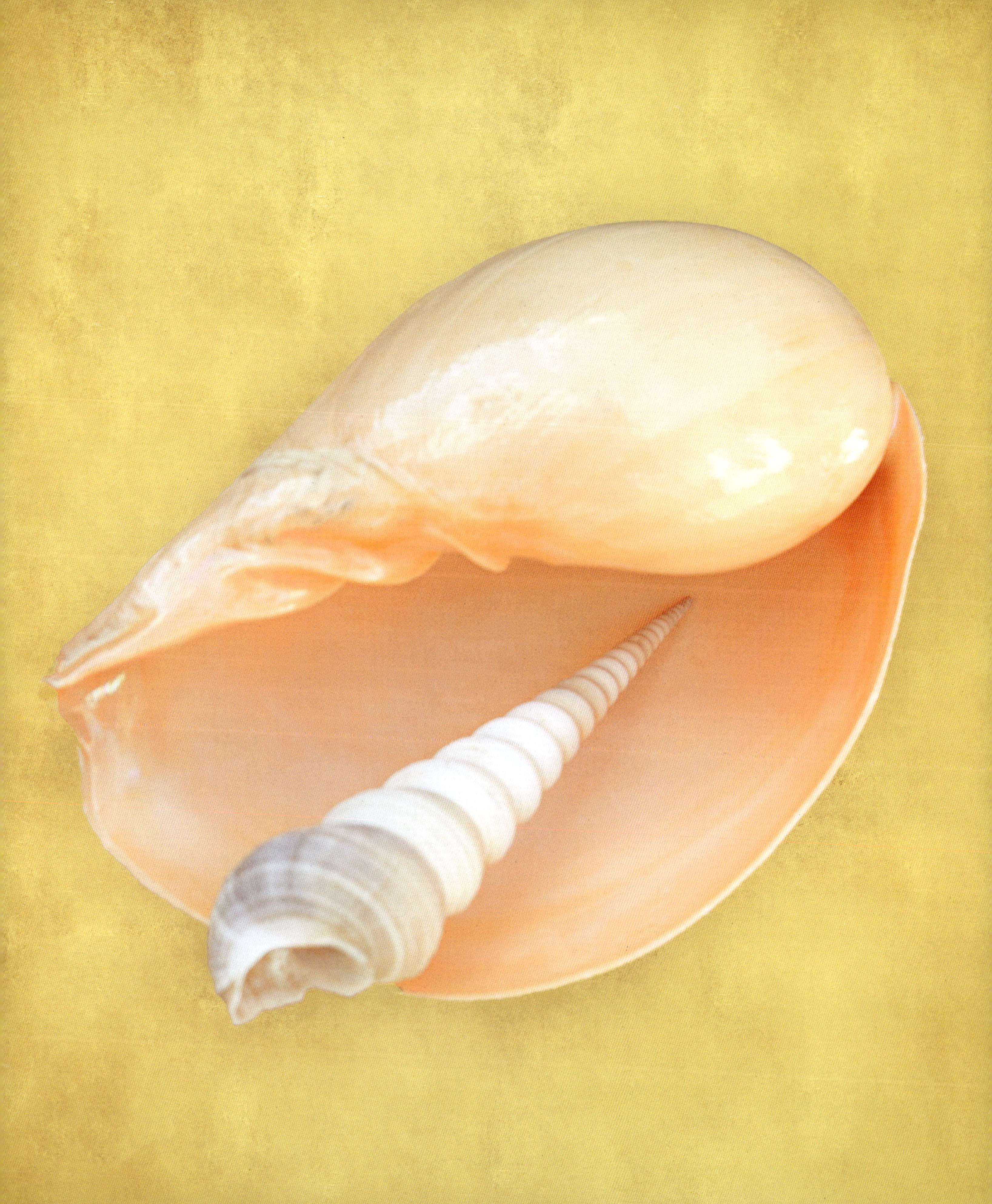

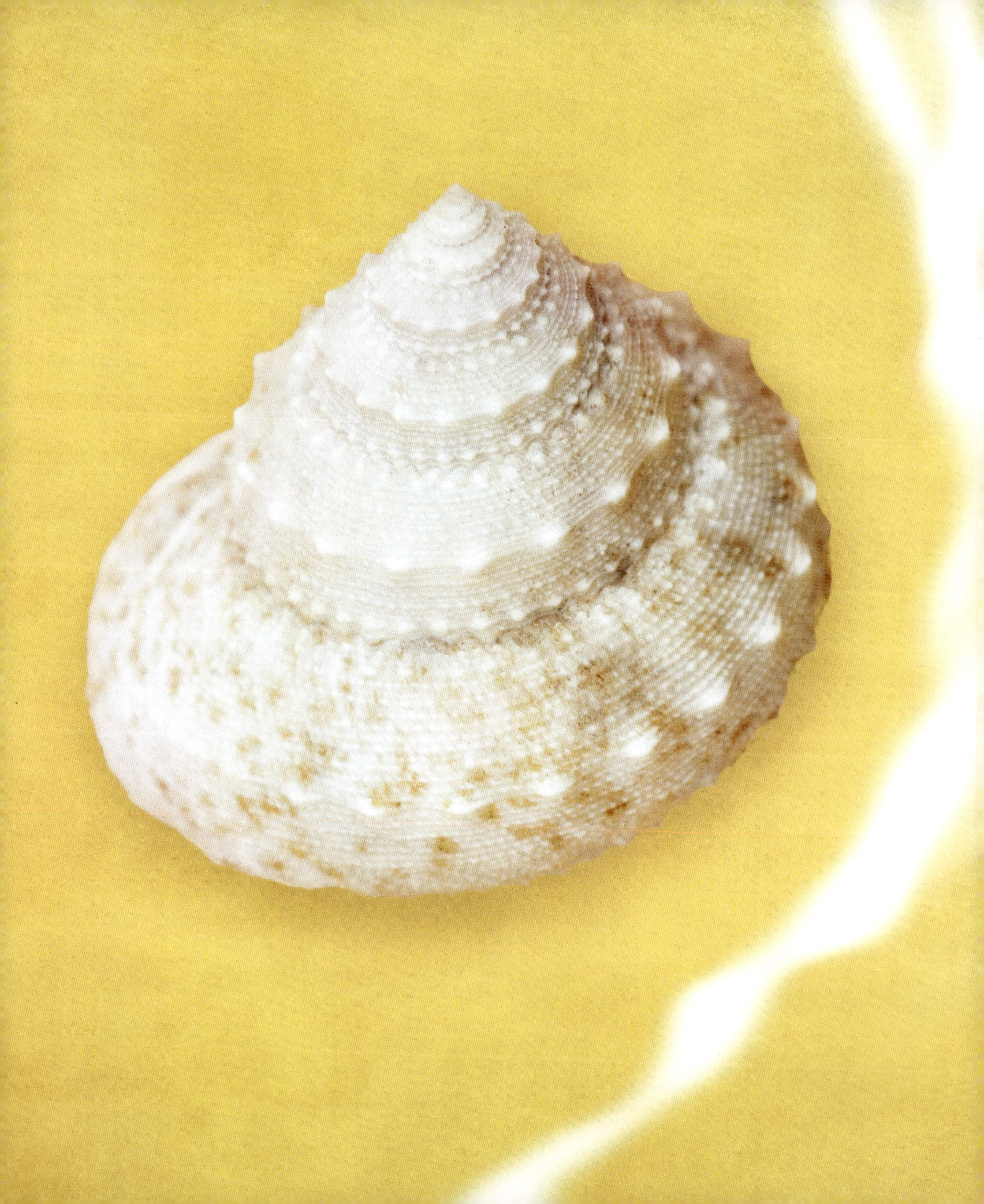

Wake at dawn with a winged heart and give thanks.

—Kahlil Gibran

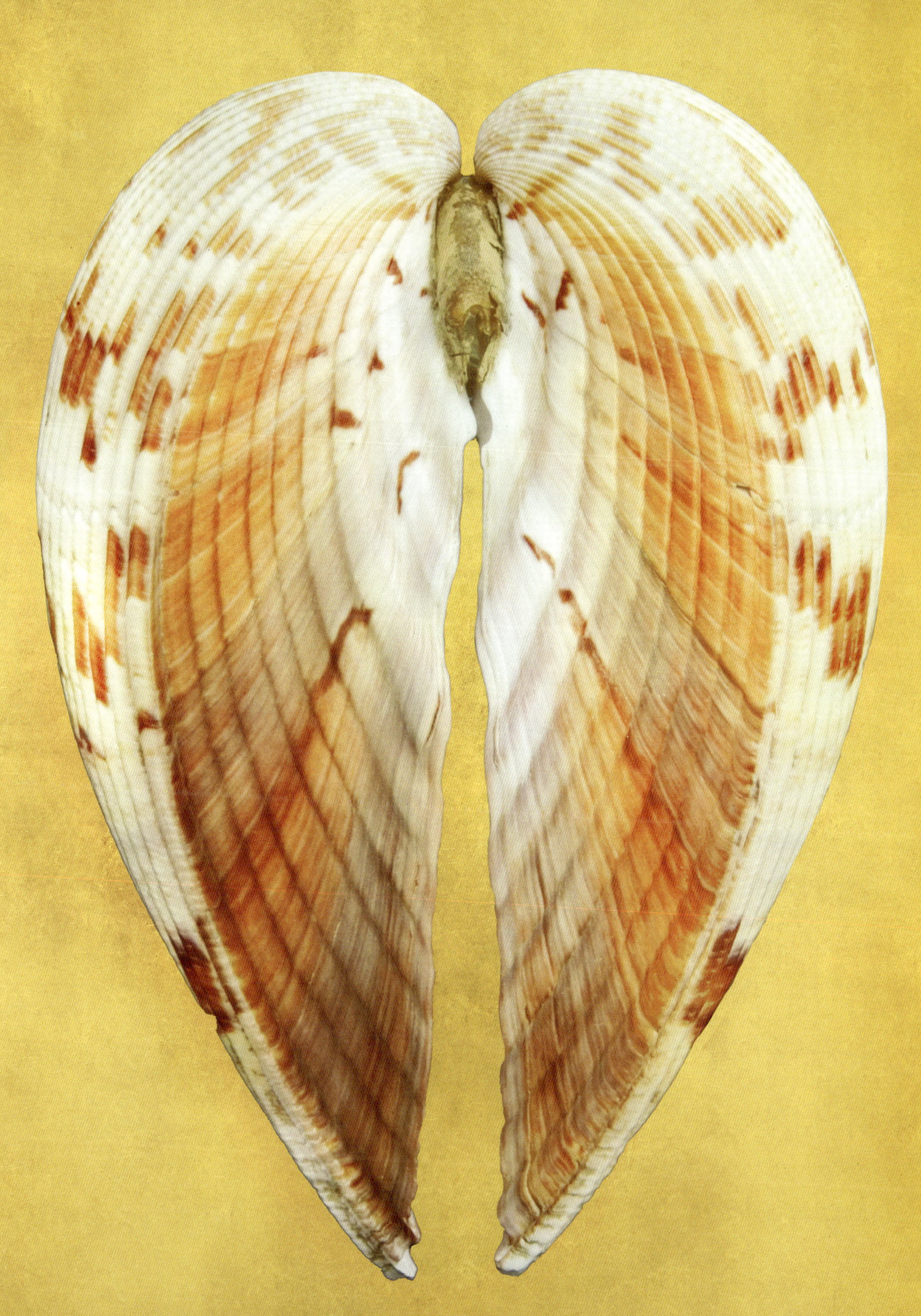

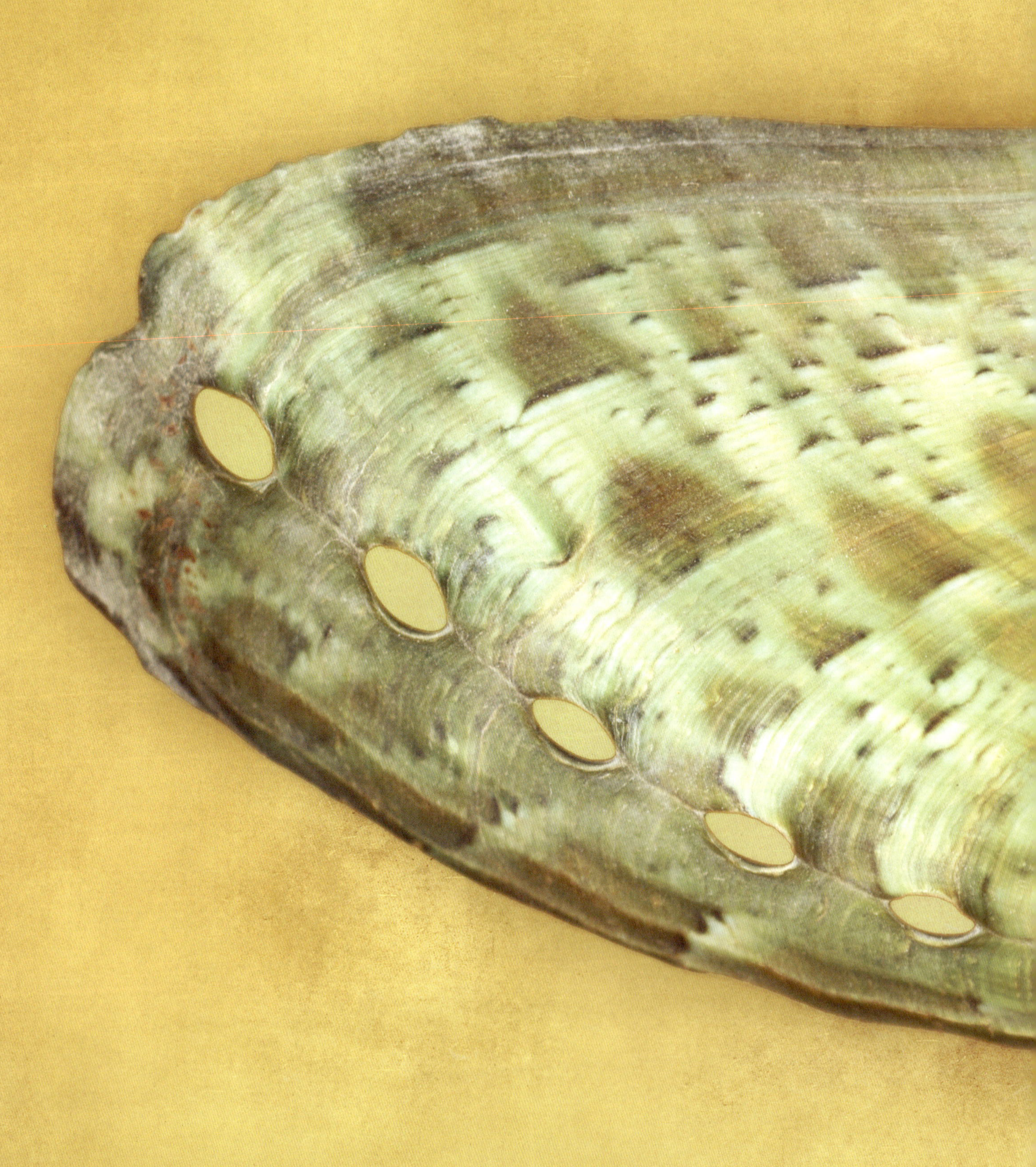

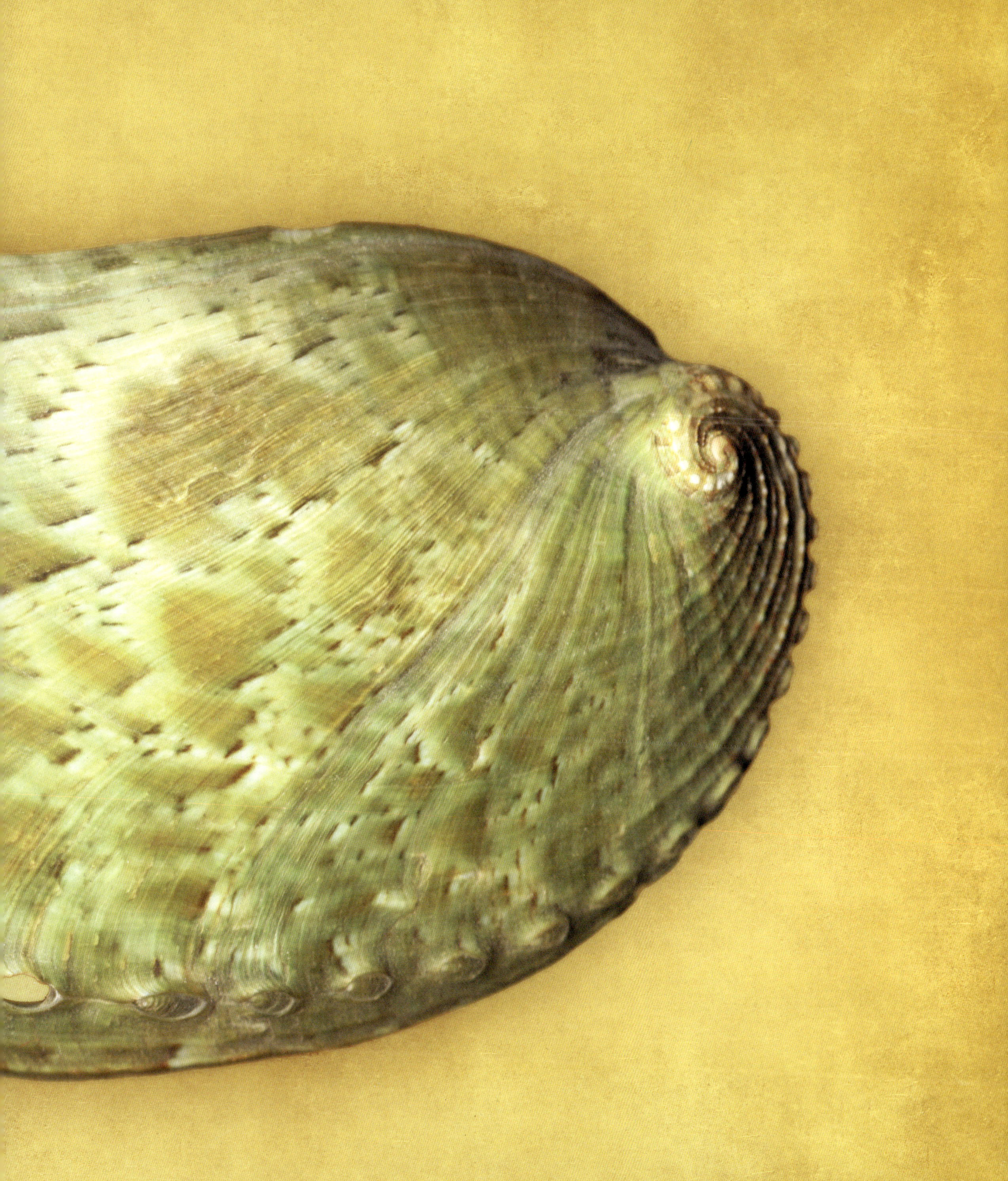

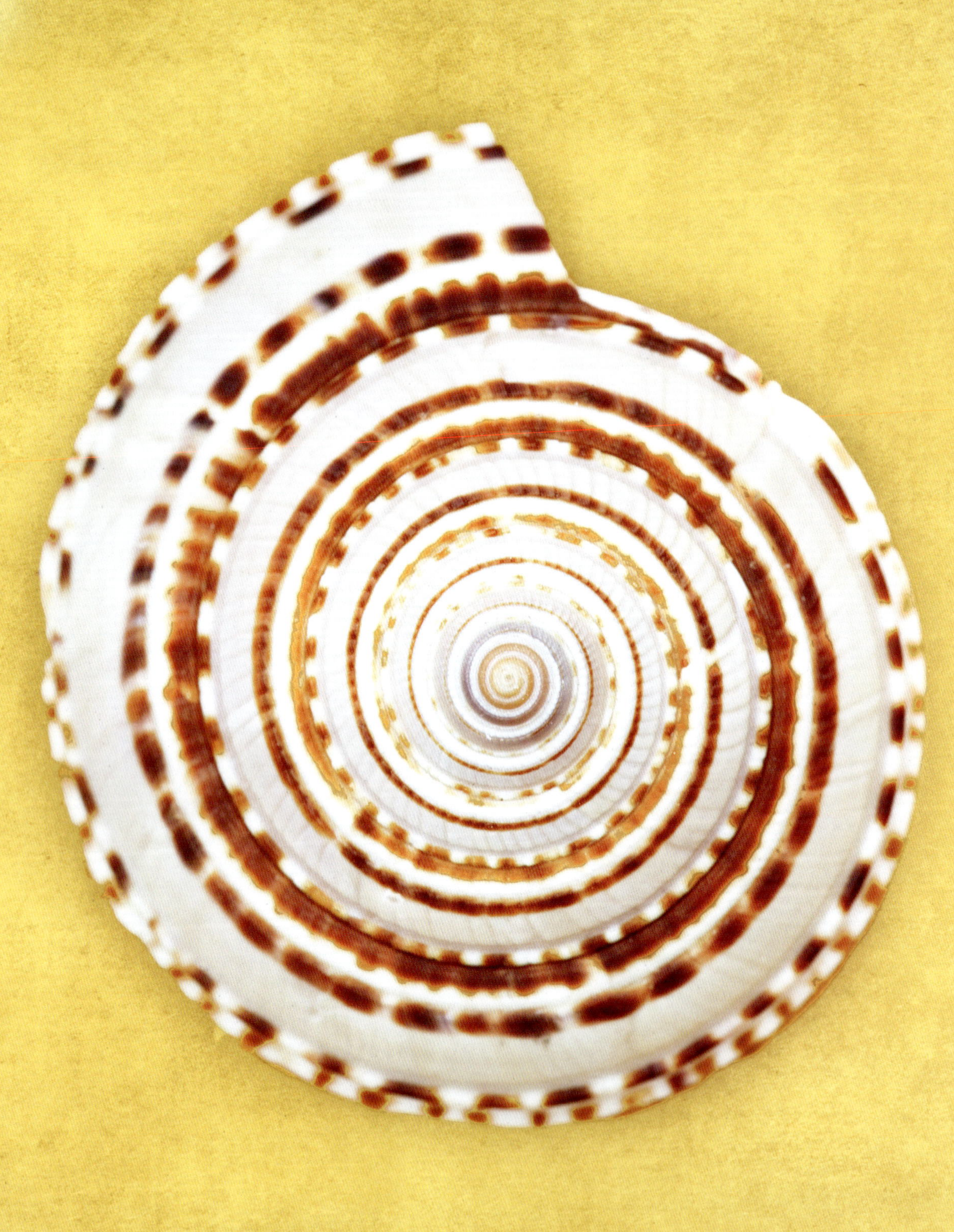

It is with colour that you render light, though you must also feel this light, have it within yourself.

—Henri Matisse

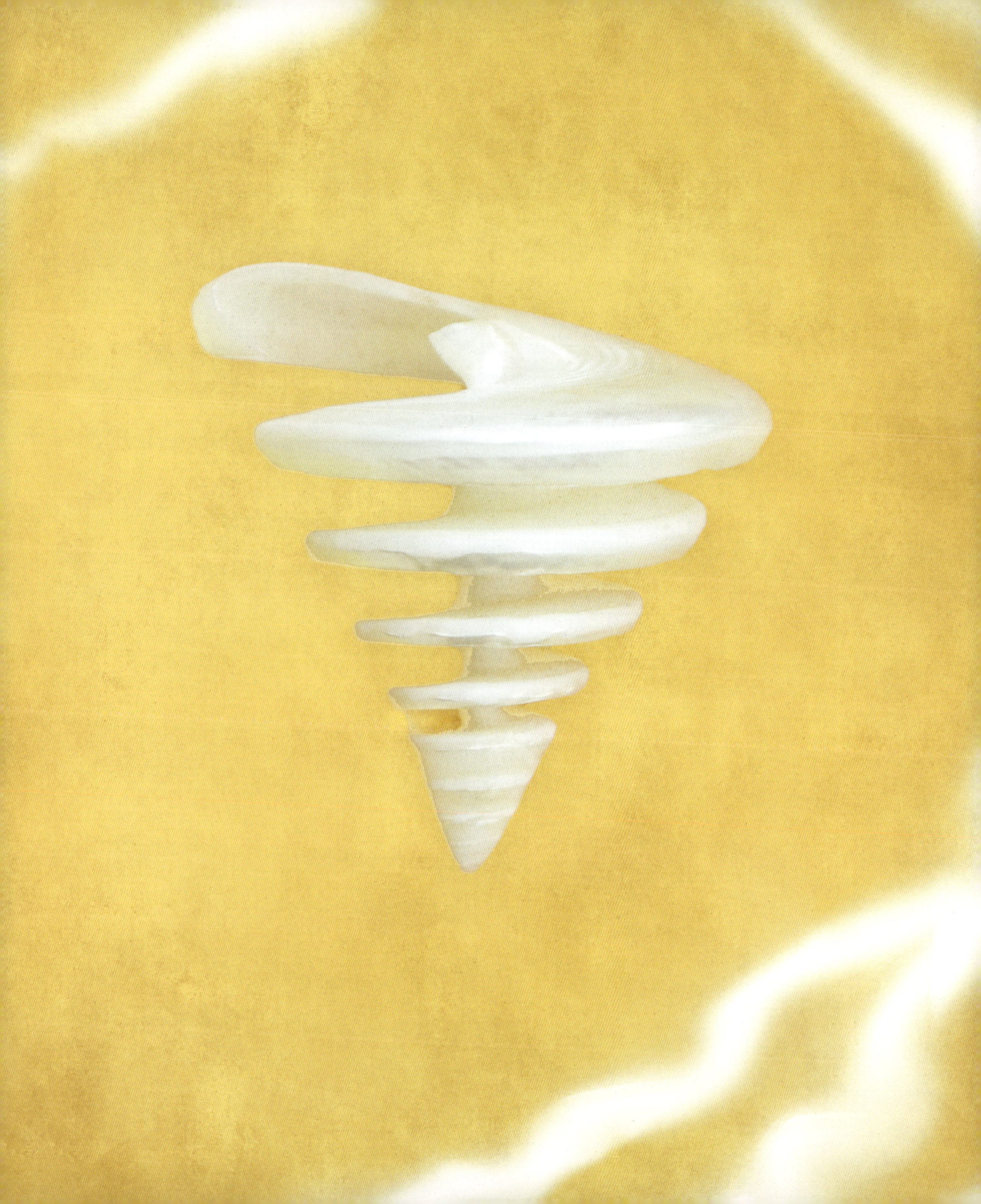

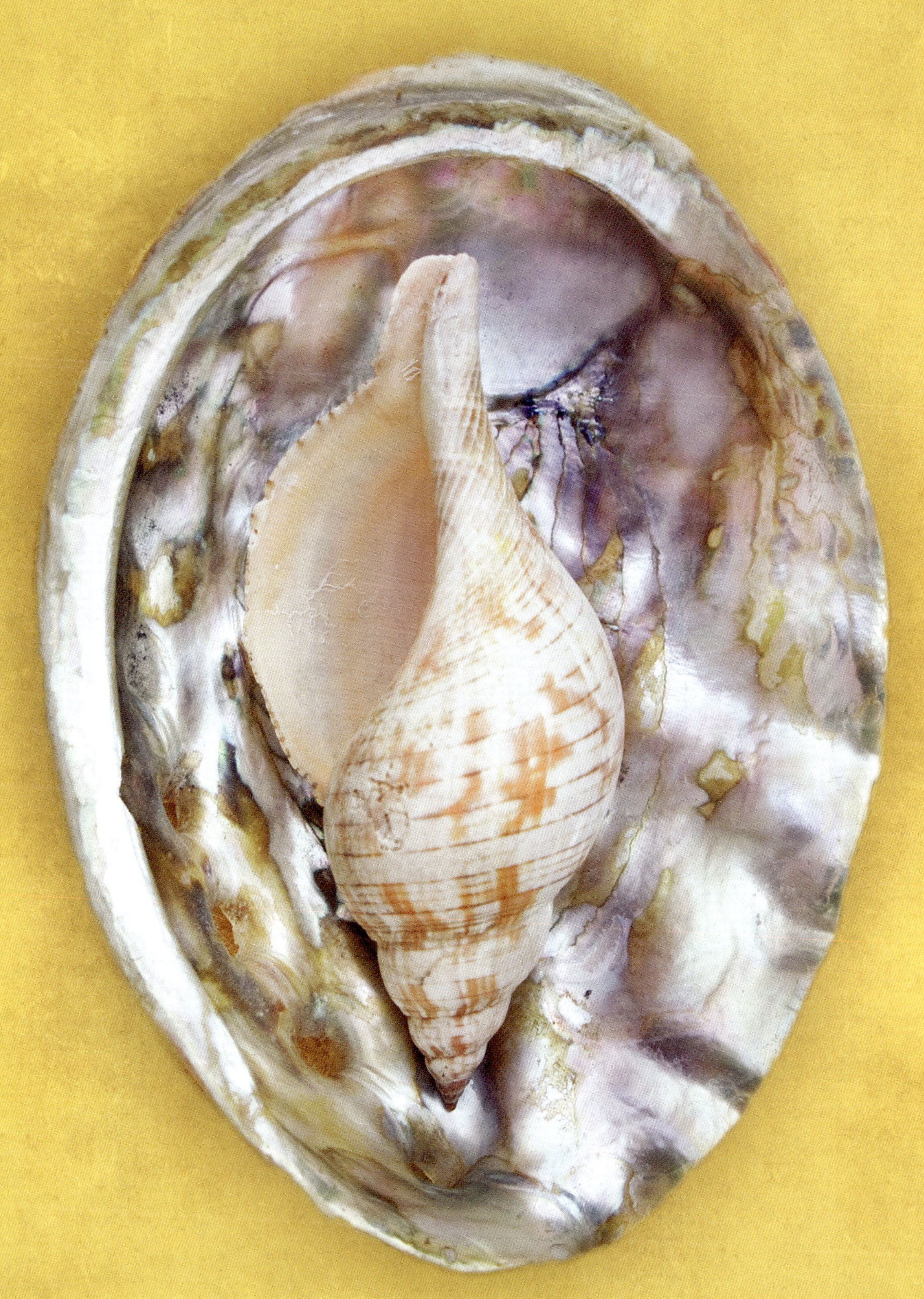

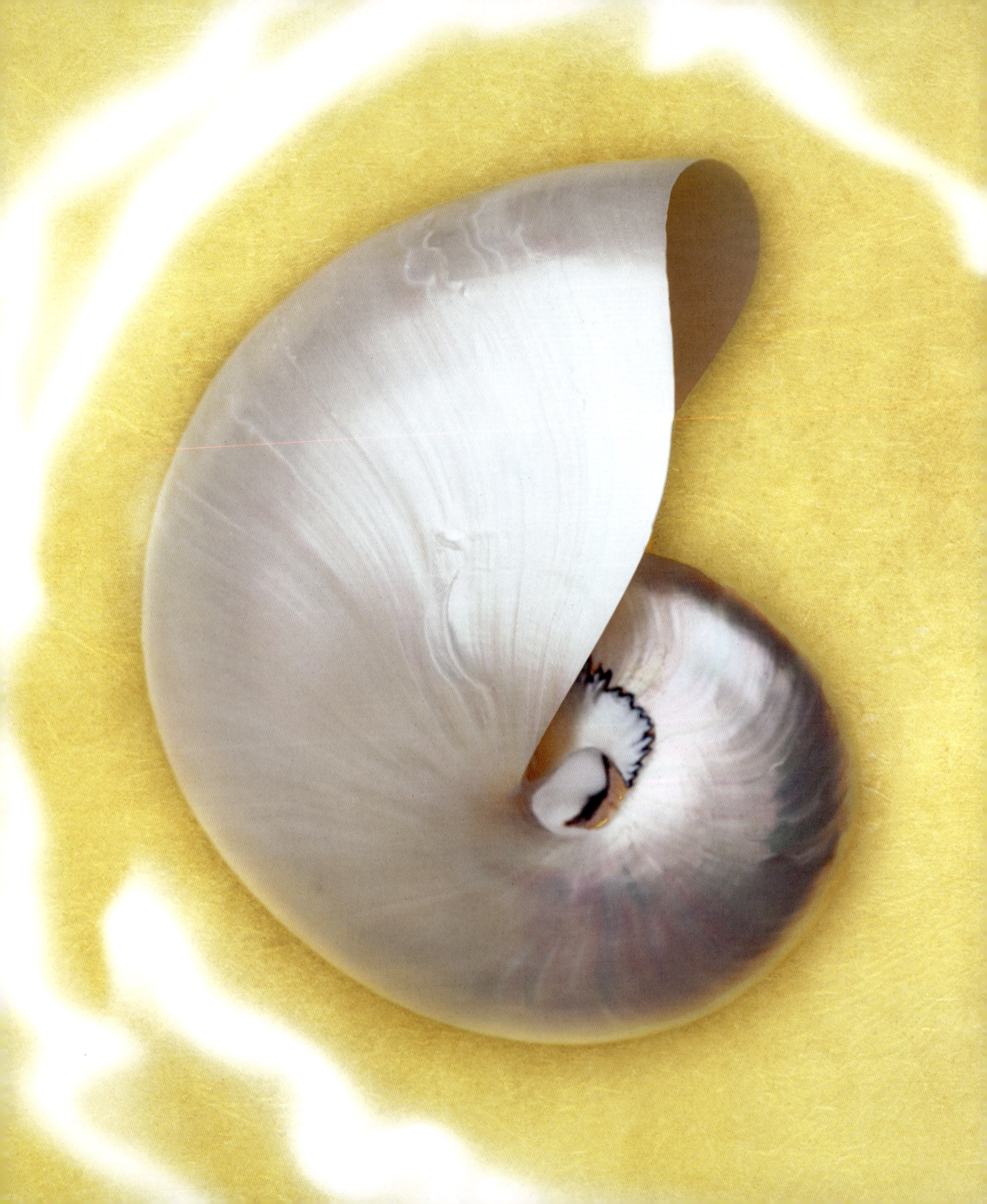

Every action of our lives touches on some chord that will vibrate in eternity.

—Sean O'Casey

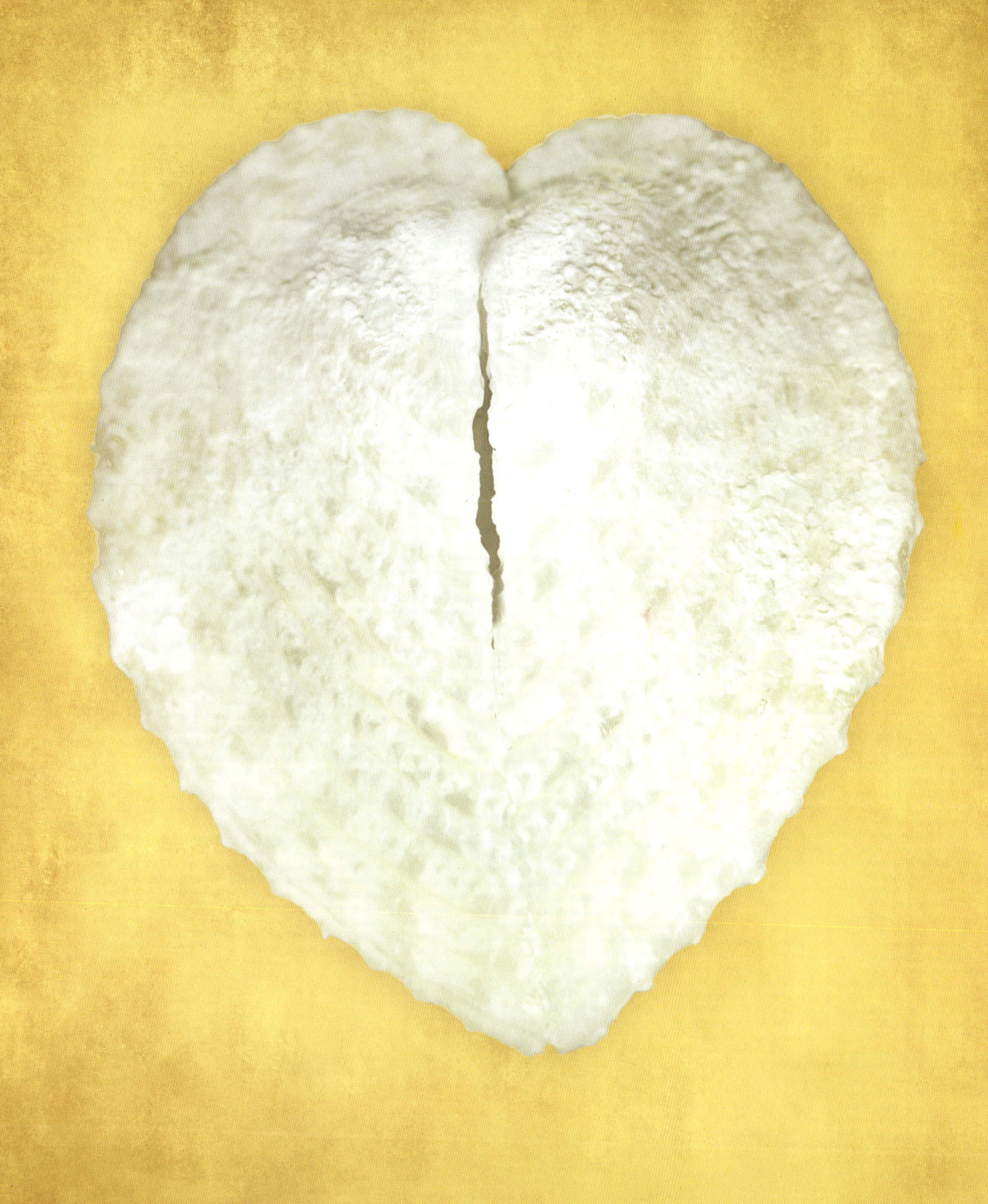

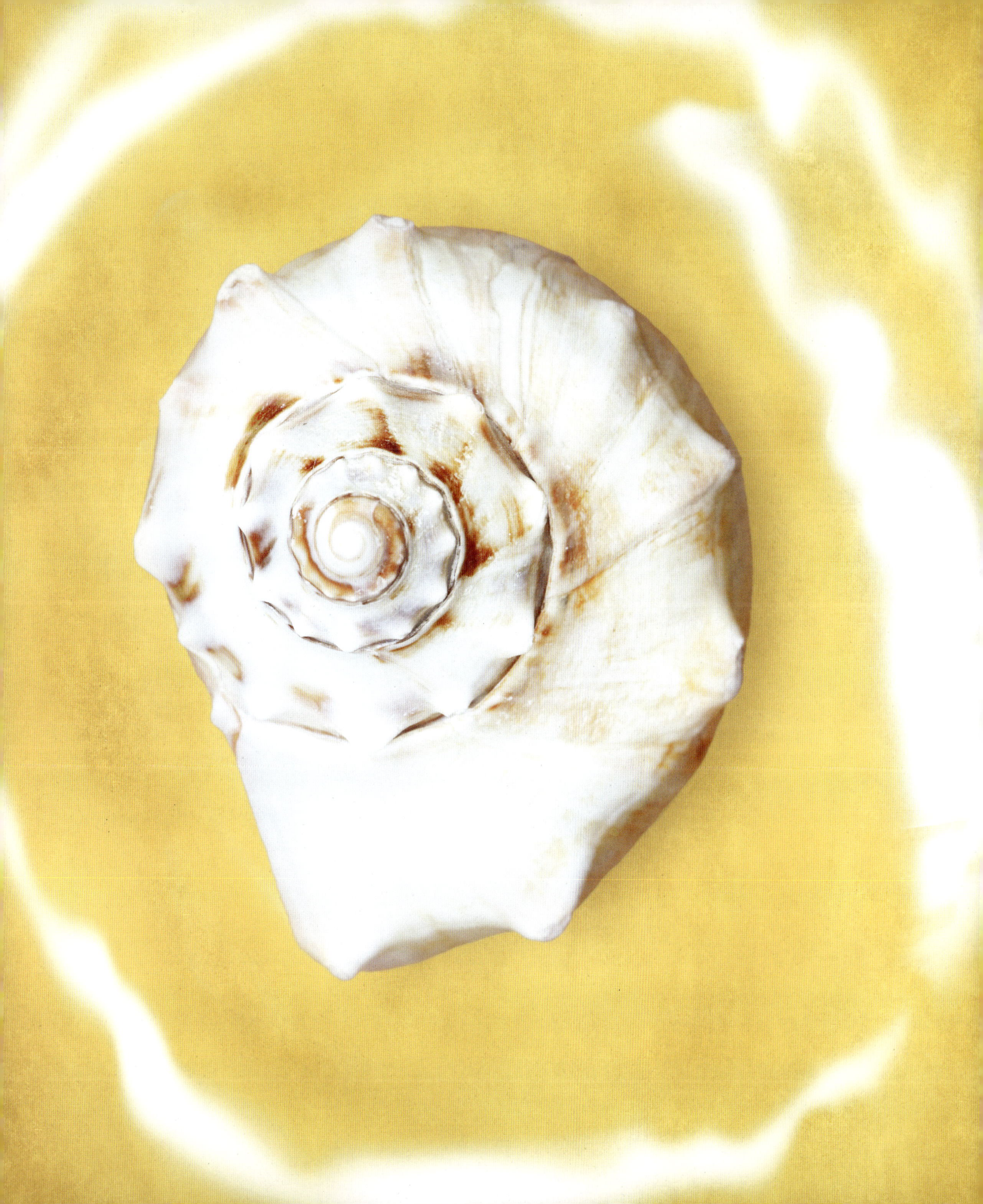

Your sacred space is where you
can find yourself again and again.

—Joseph Campbell

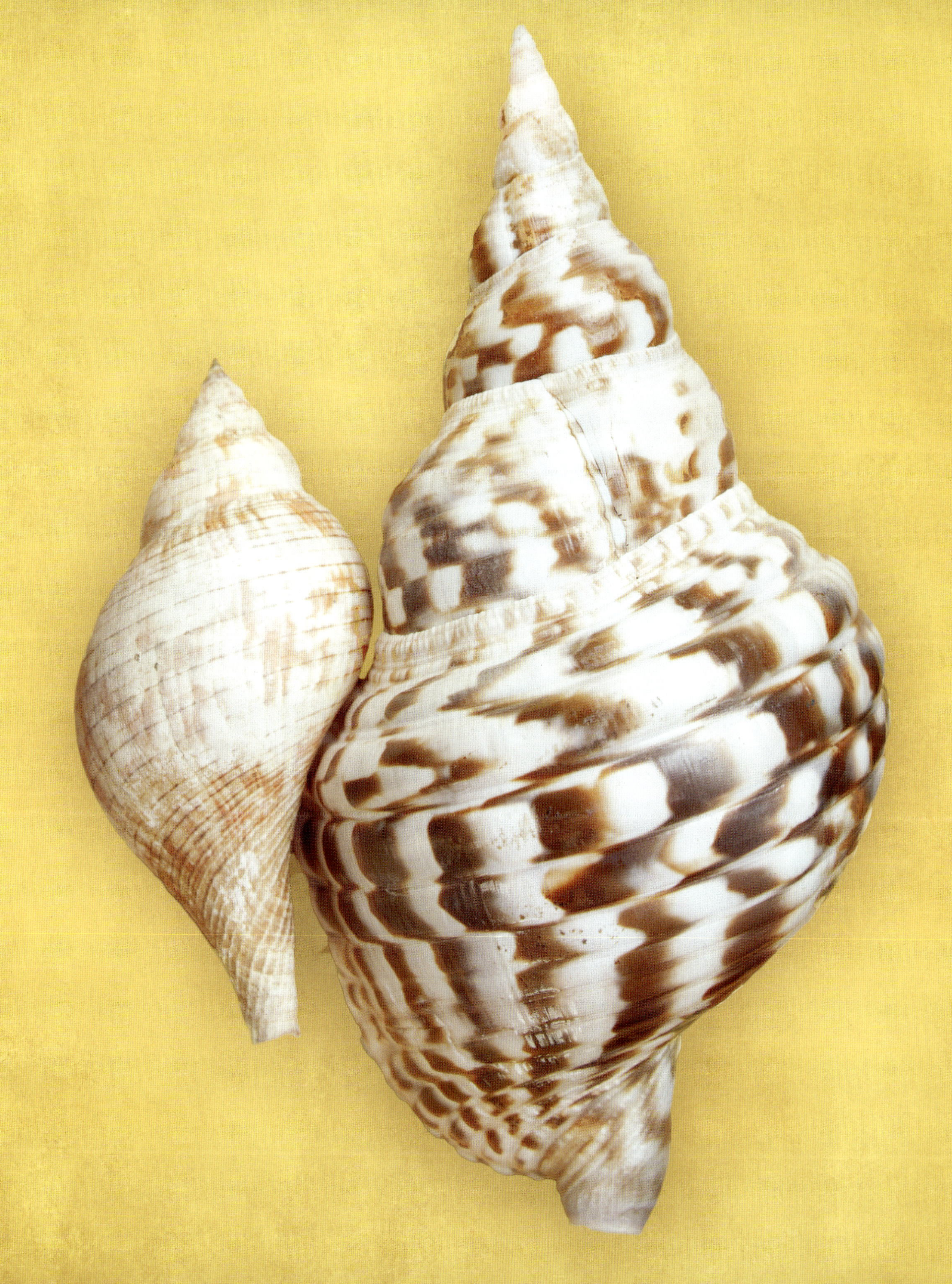

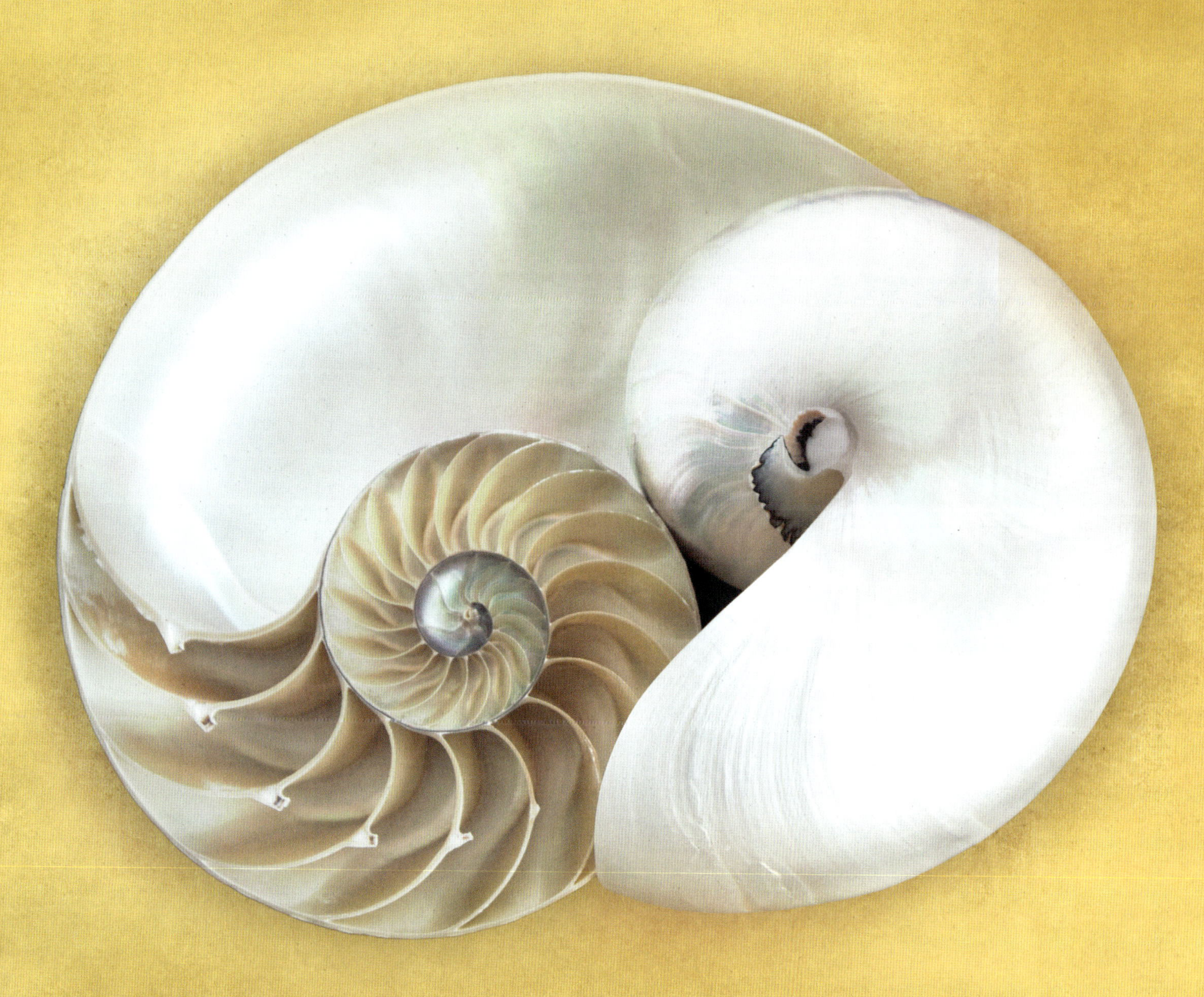

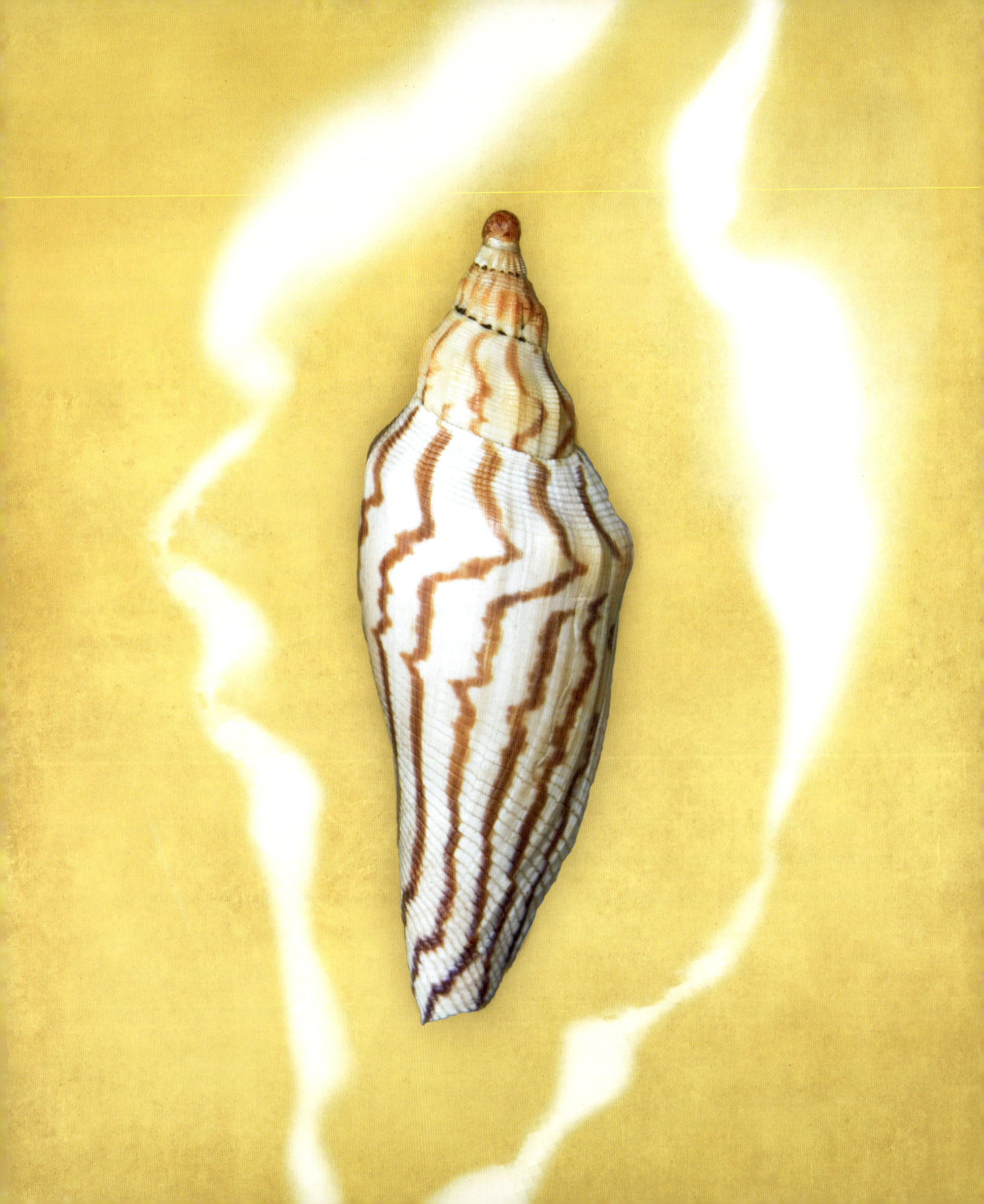

Sometimes our light goes out but is blown into flame by another human being. Each of us owes deepest thanks to those who have rekindled this light.

—Albert Schweitzer

The possession of knowledge does not kill the sense of wonder and mystery. There is always more mystery.

—Anais Nin

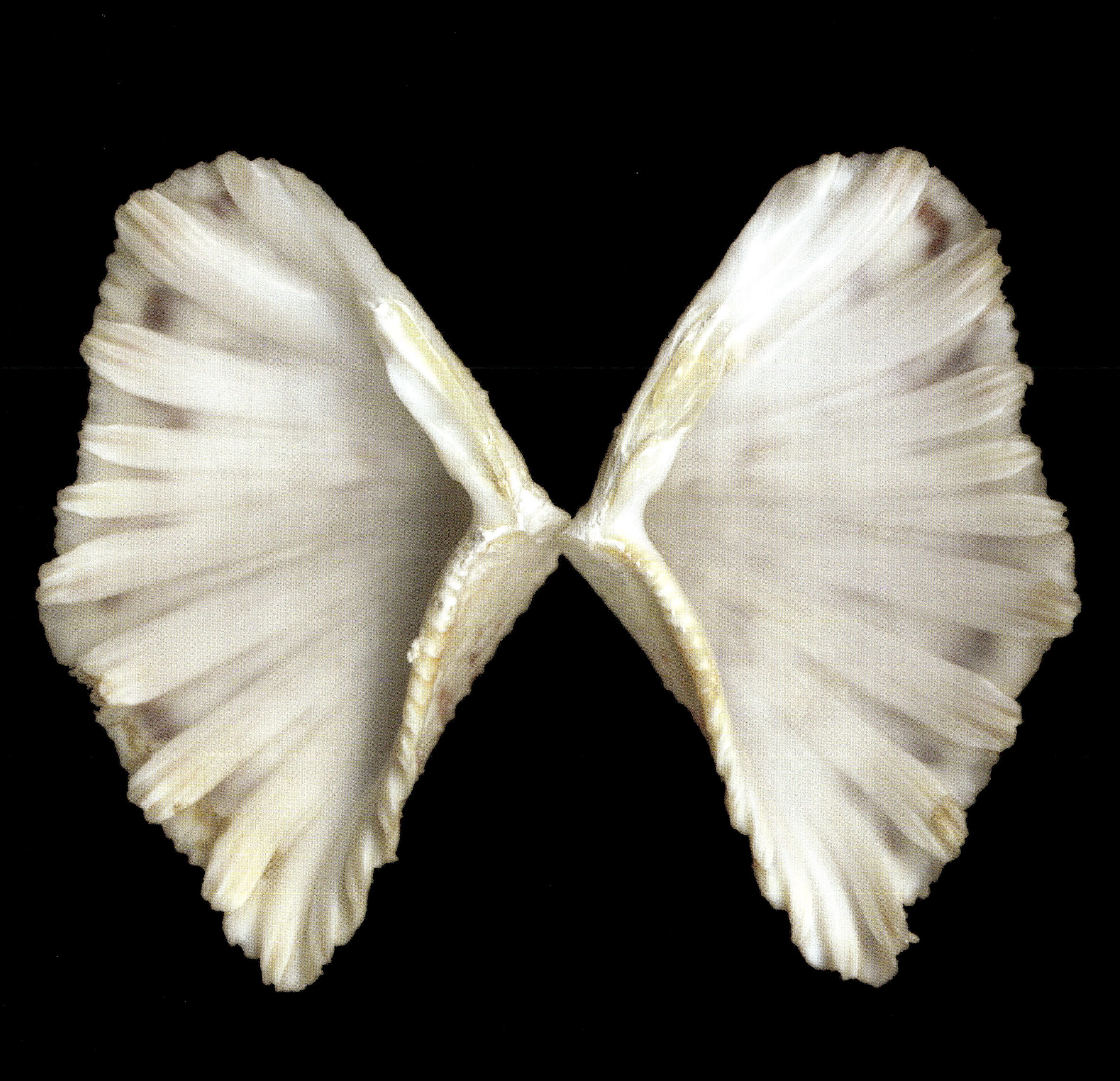

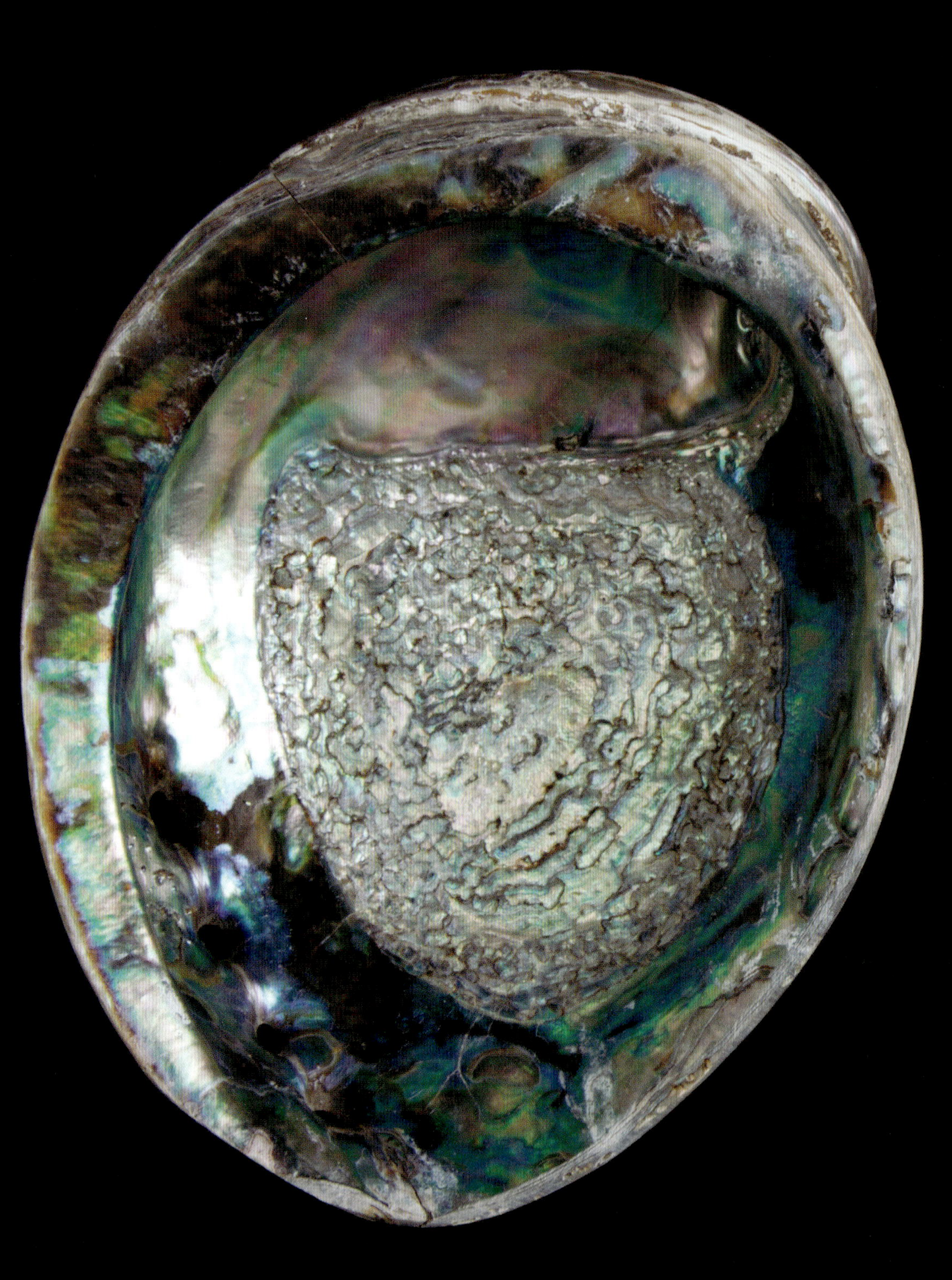

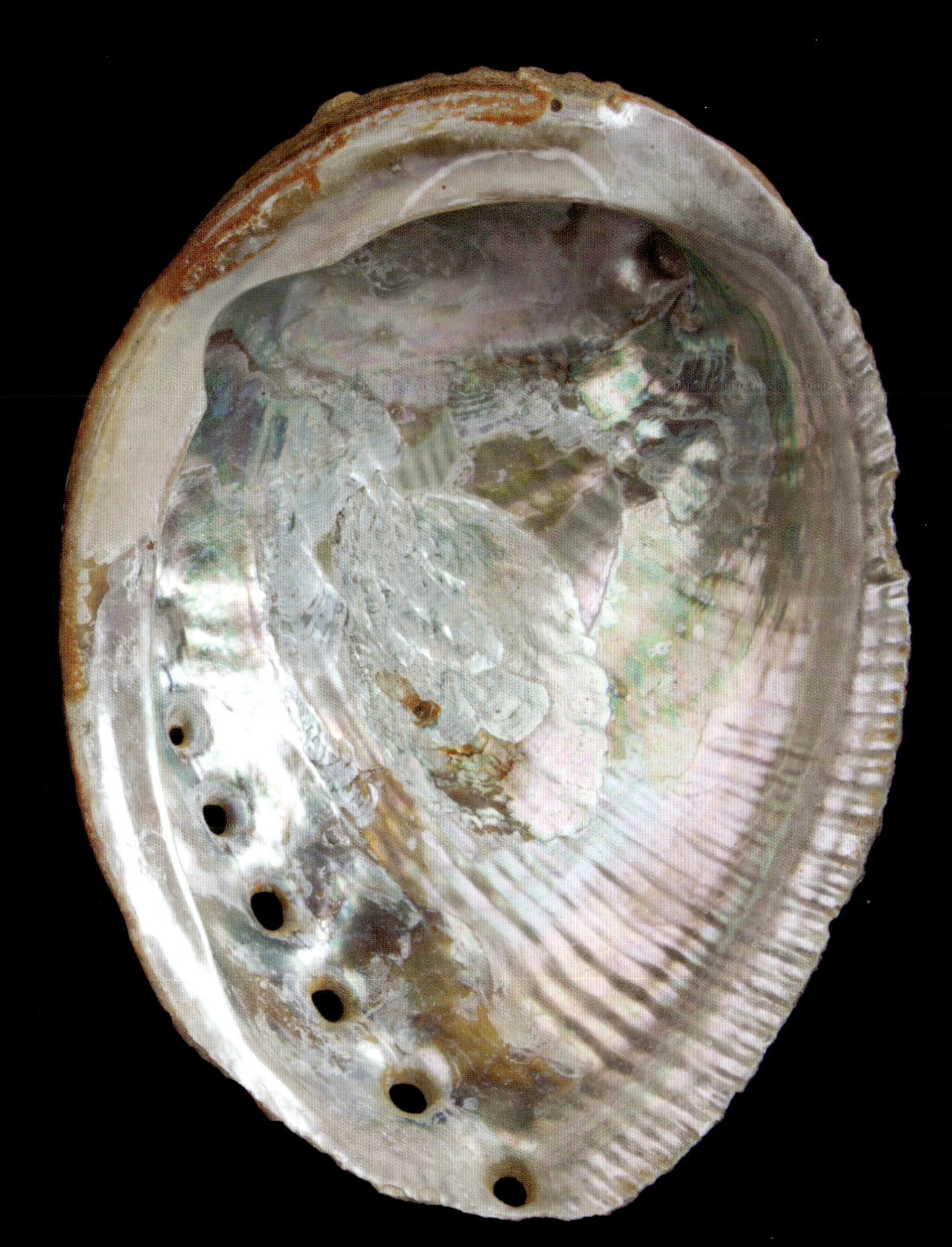

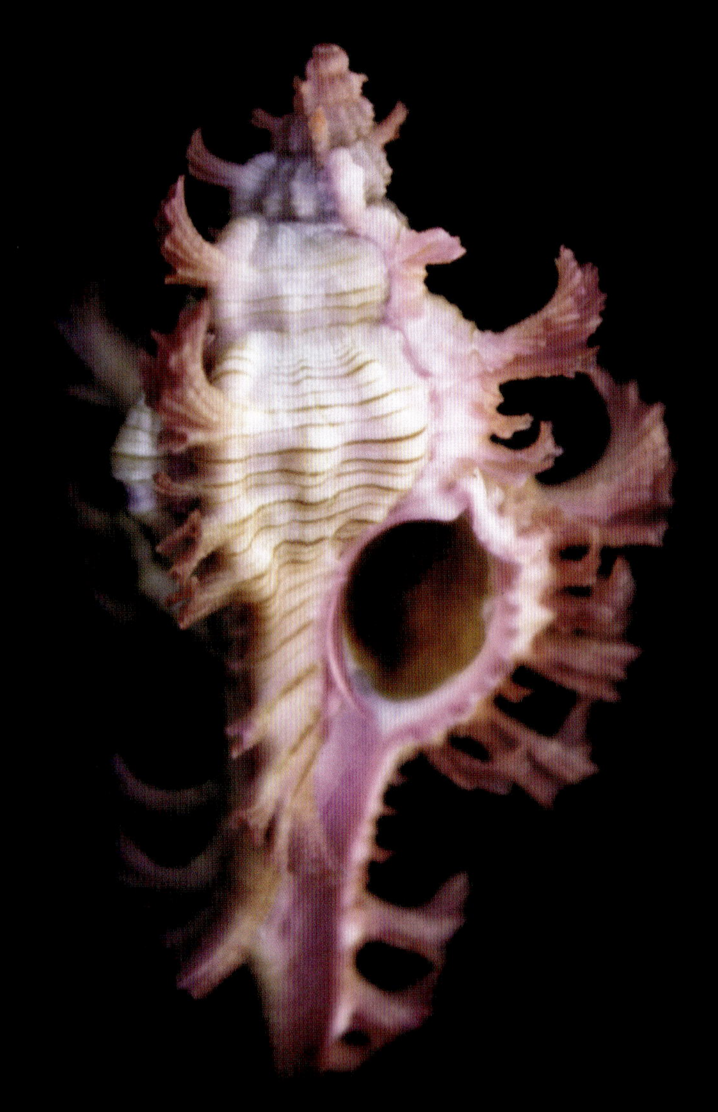

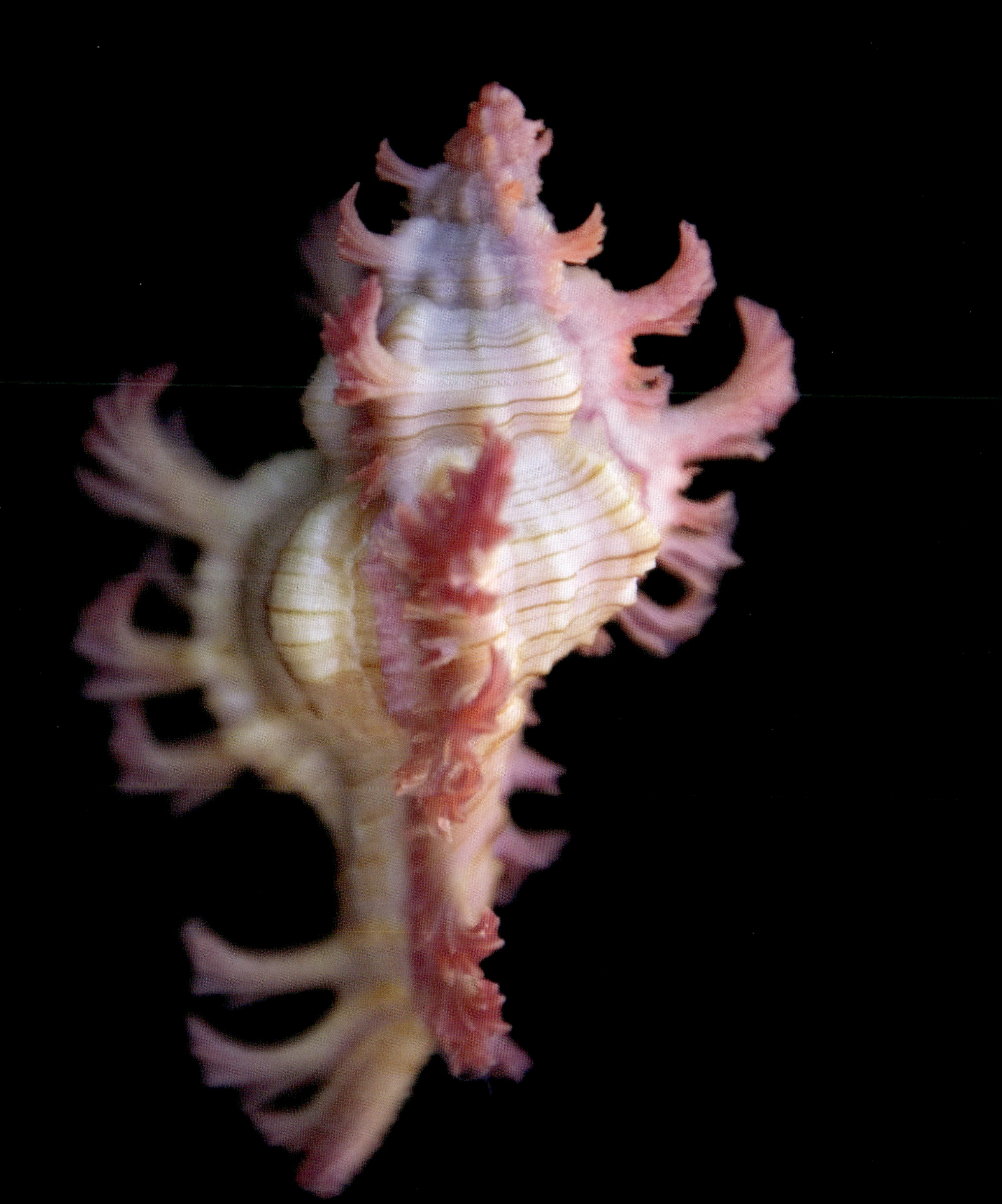

Your work is to discover your work and then with all your heart to give yourself to it.

—Buddha

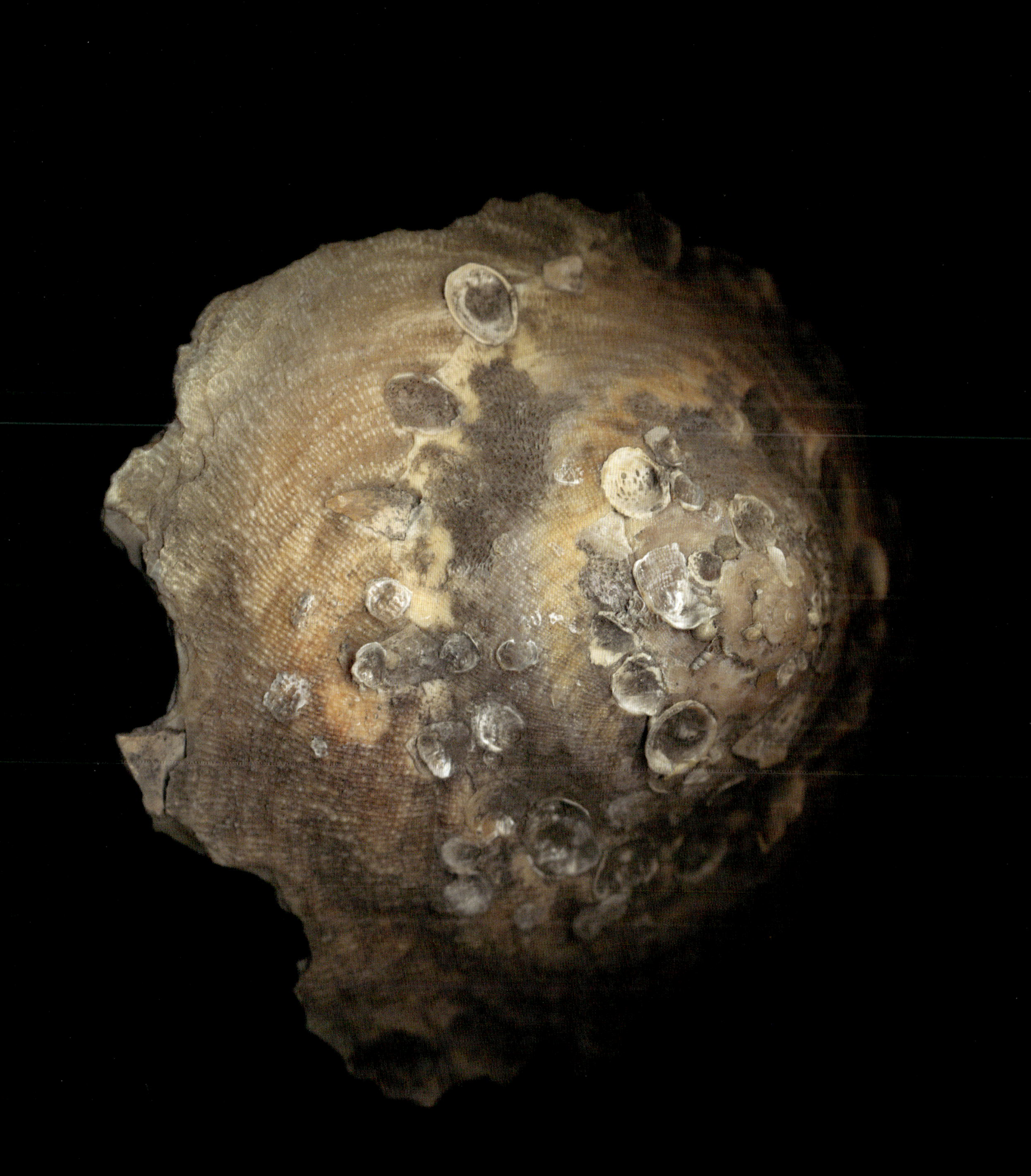

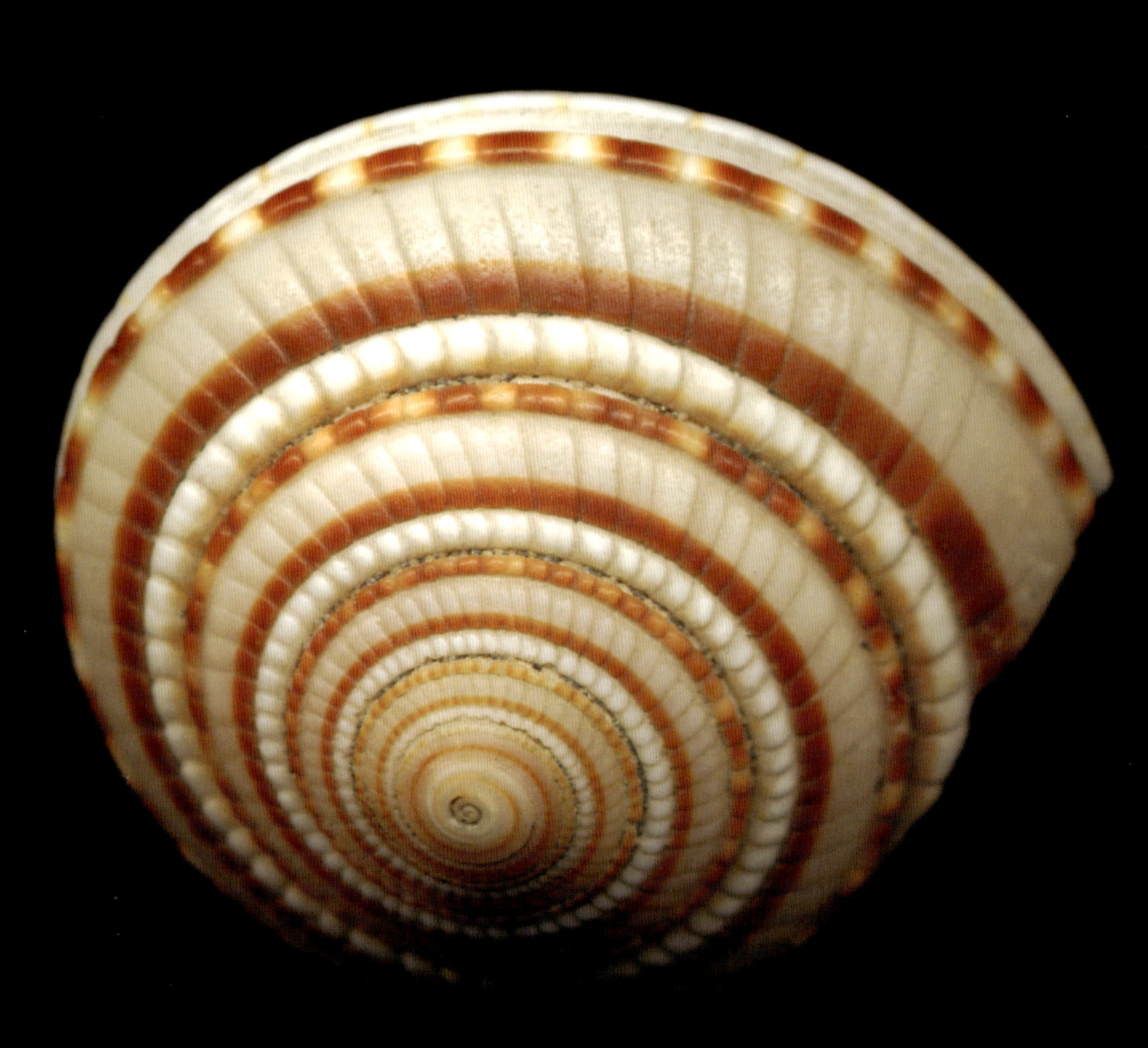

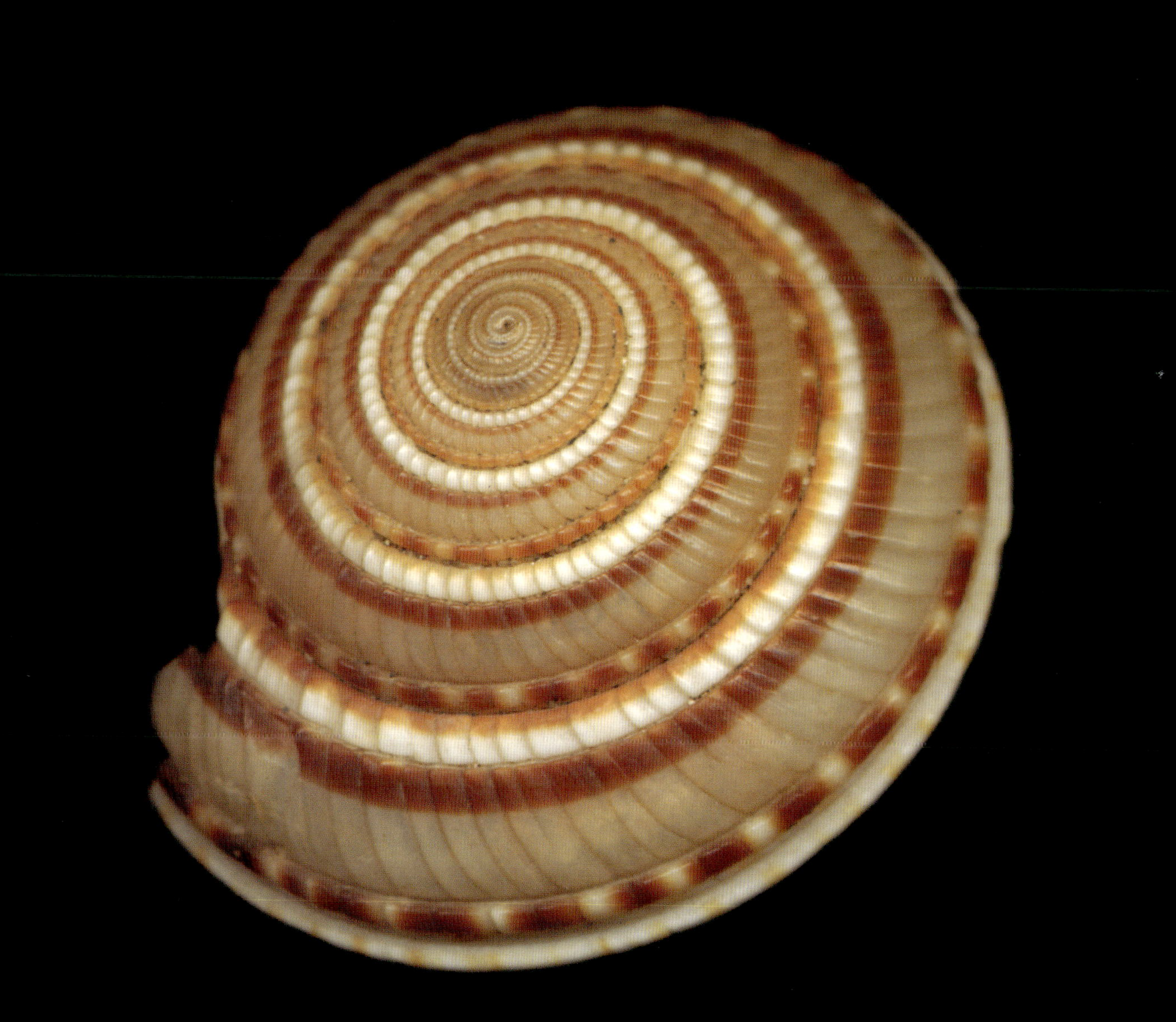

*Deep into that darkness peering, long I stood there,
wondering, fearing, doubting, dreaming dreams
no mortal ever dared to dream before.*

—Edgar Allan Poe

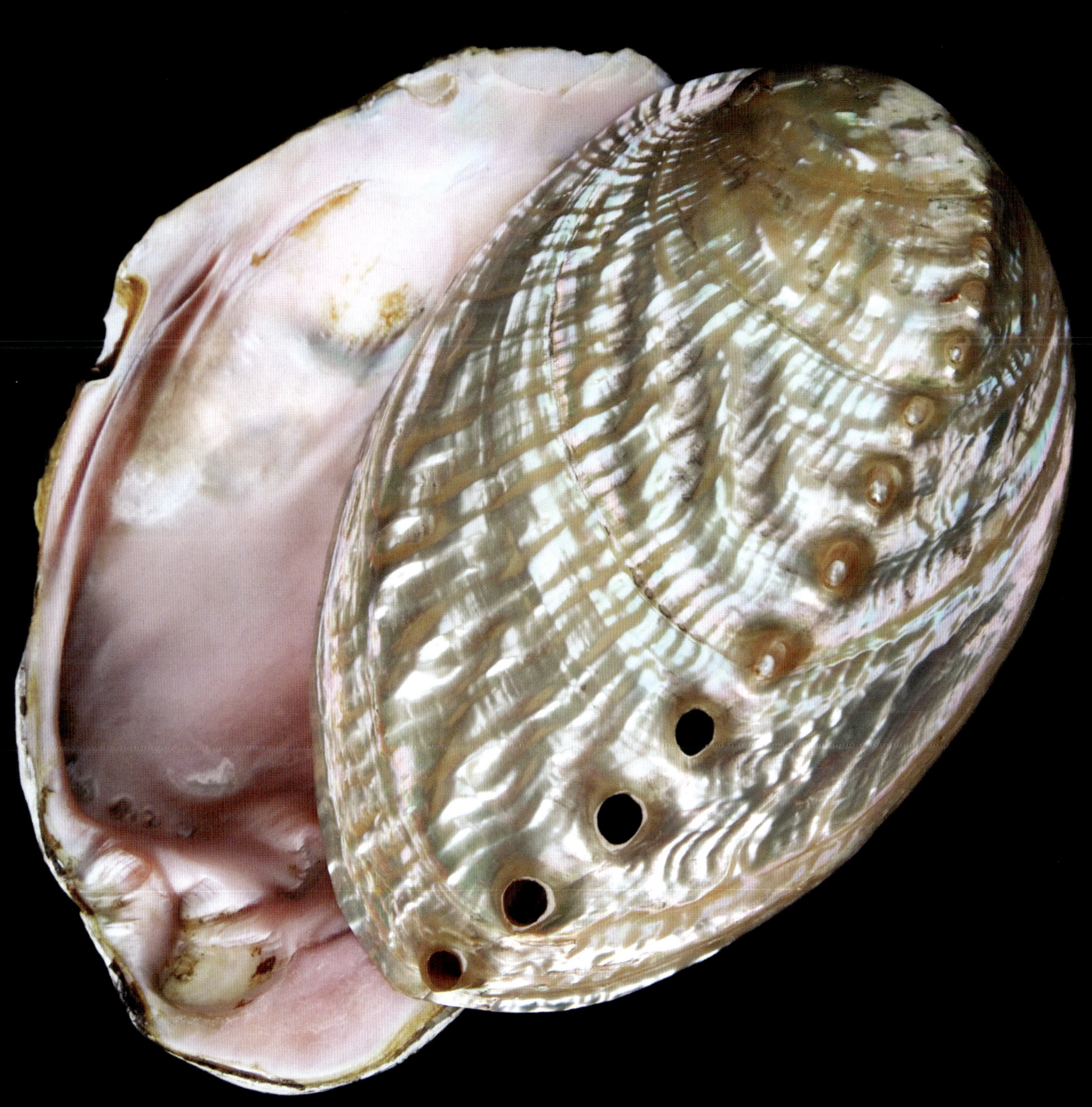

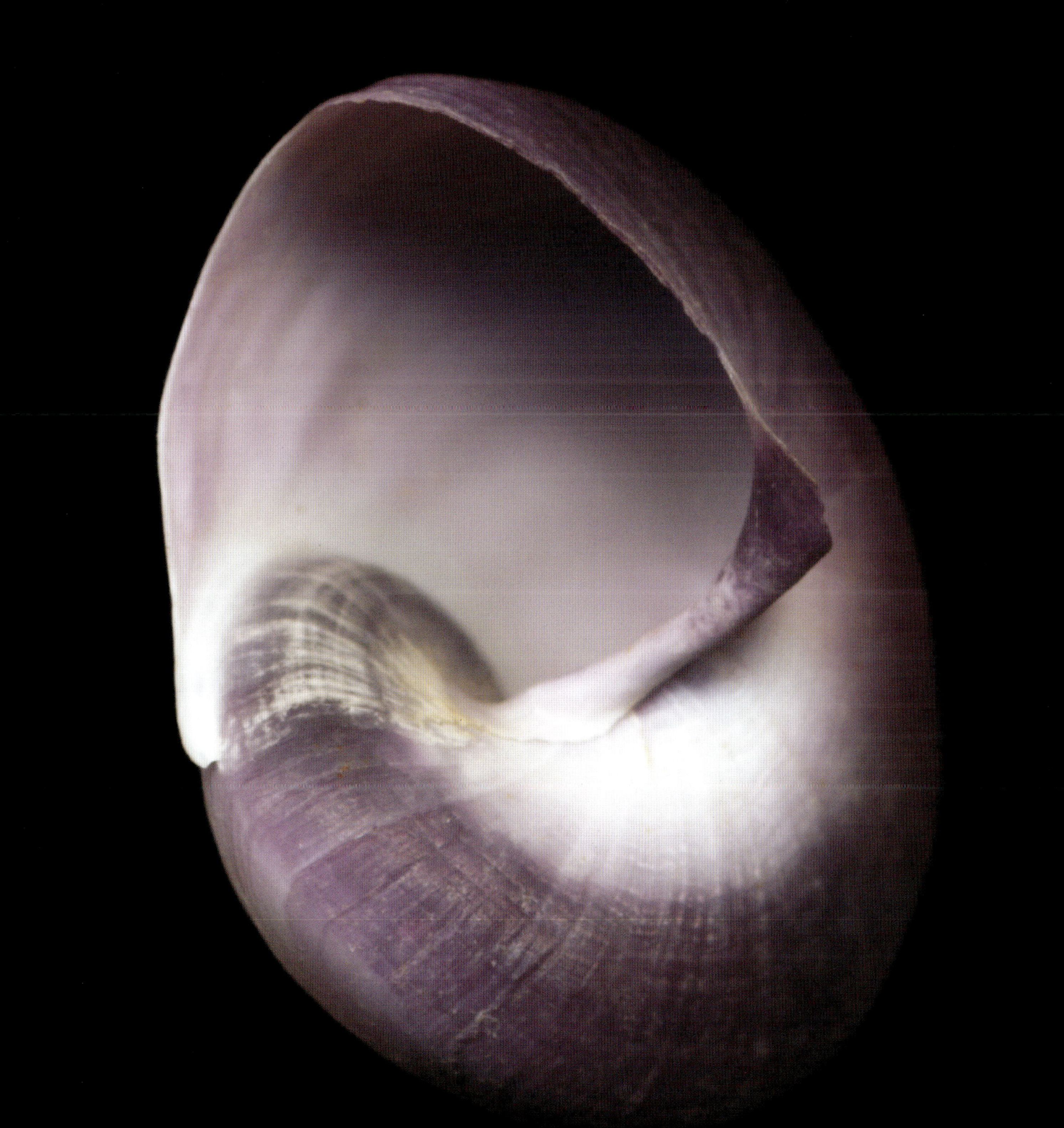

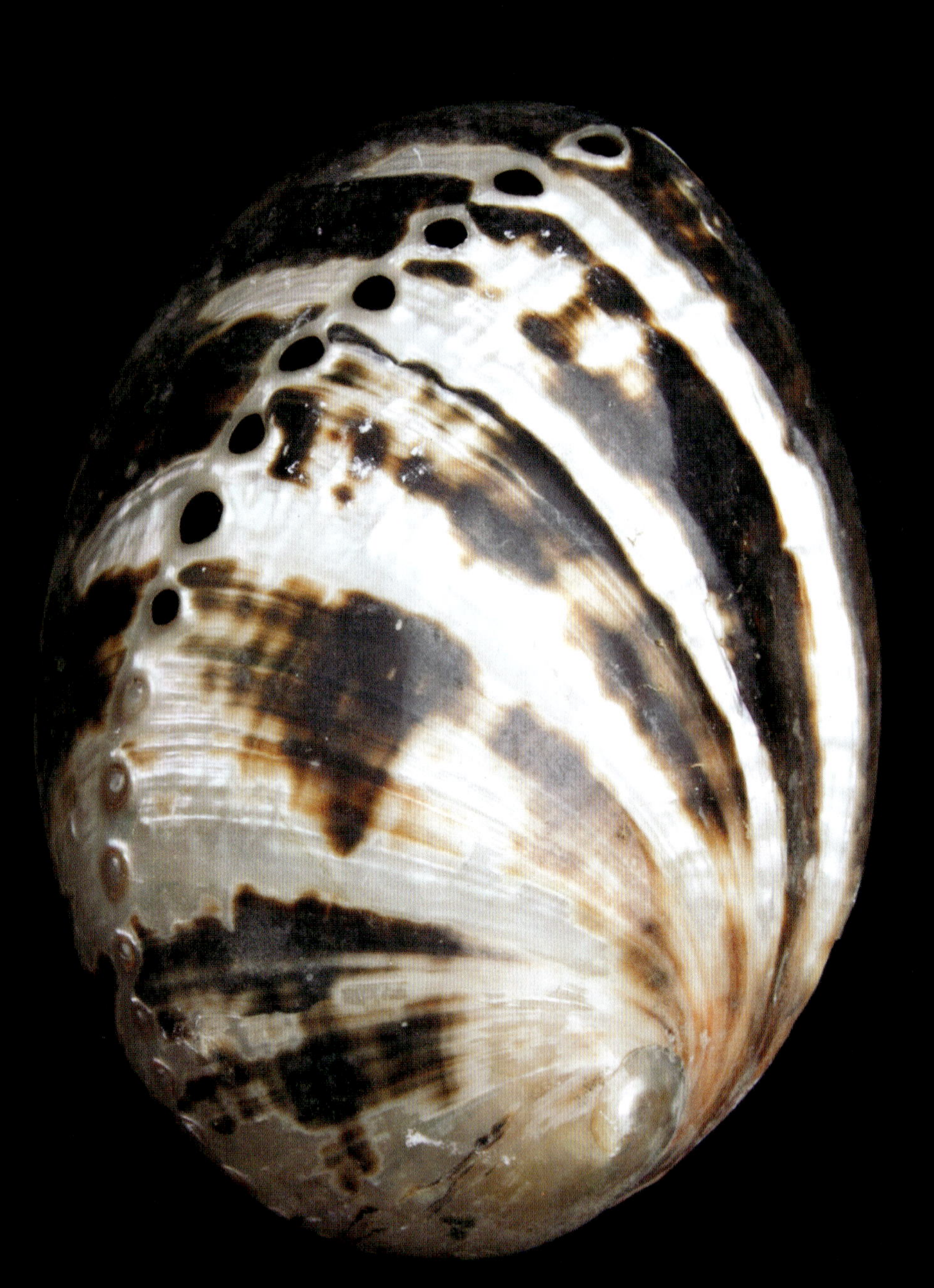

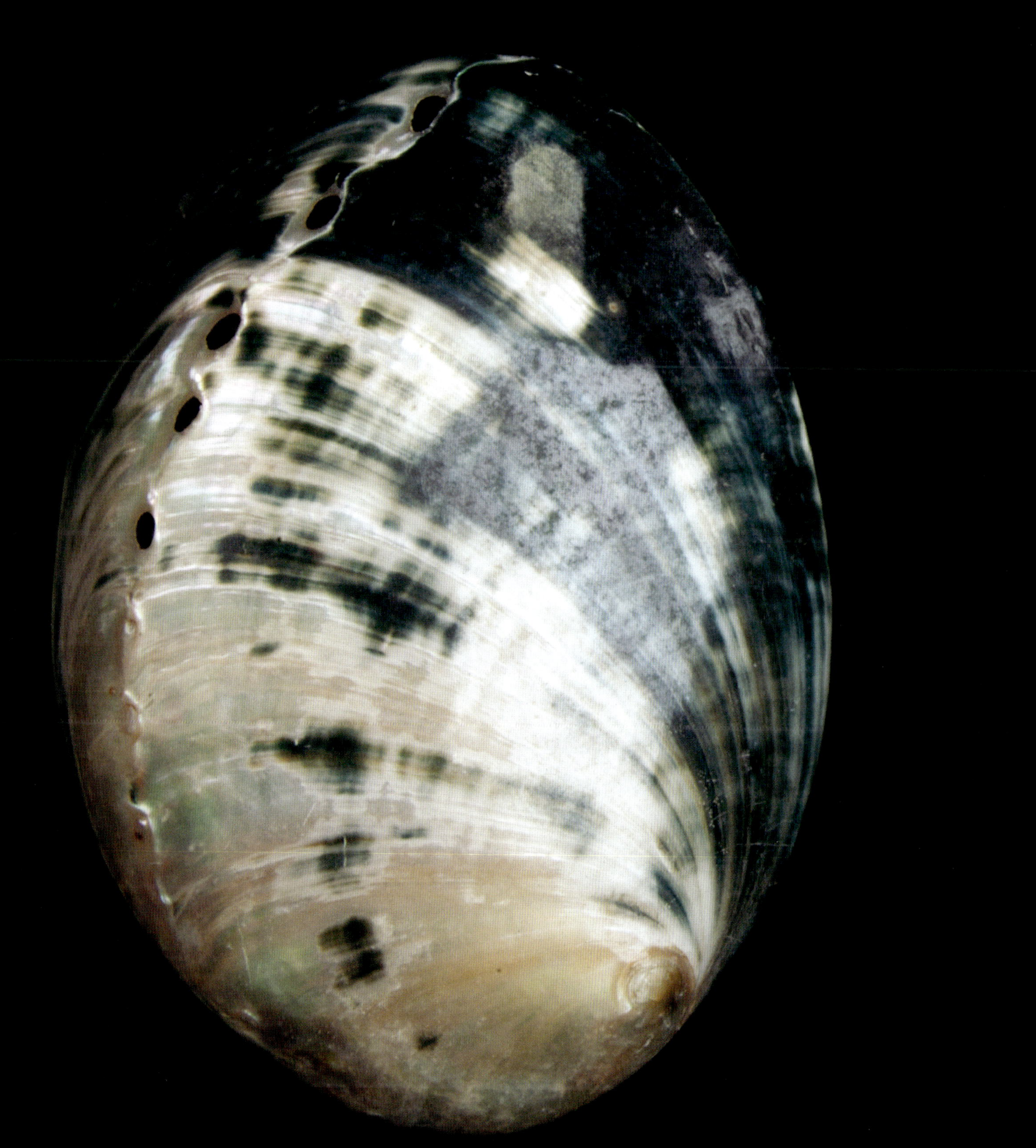

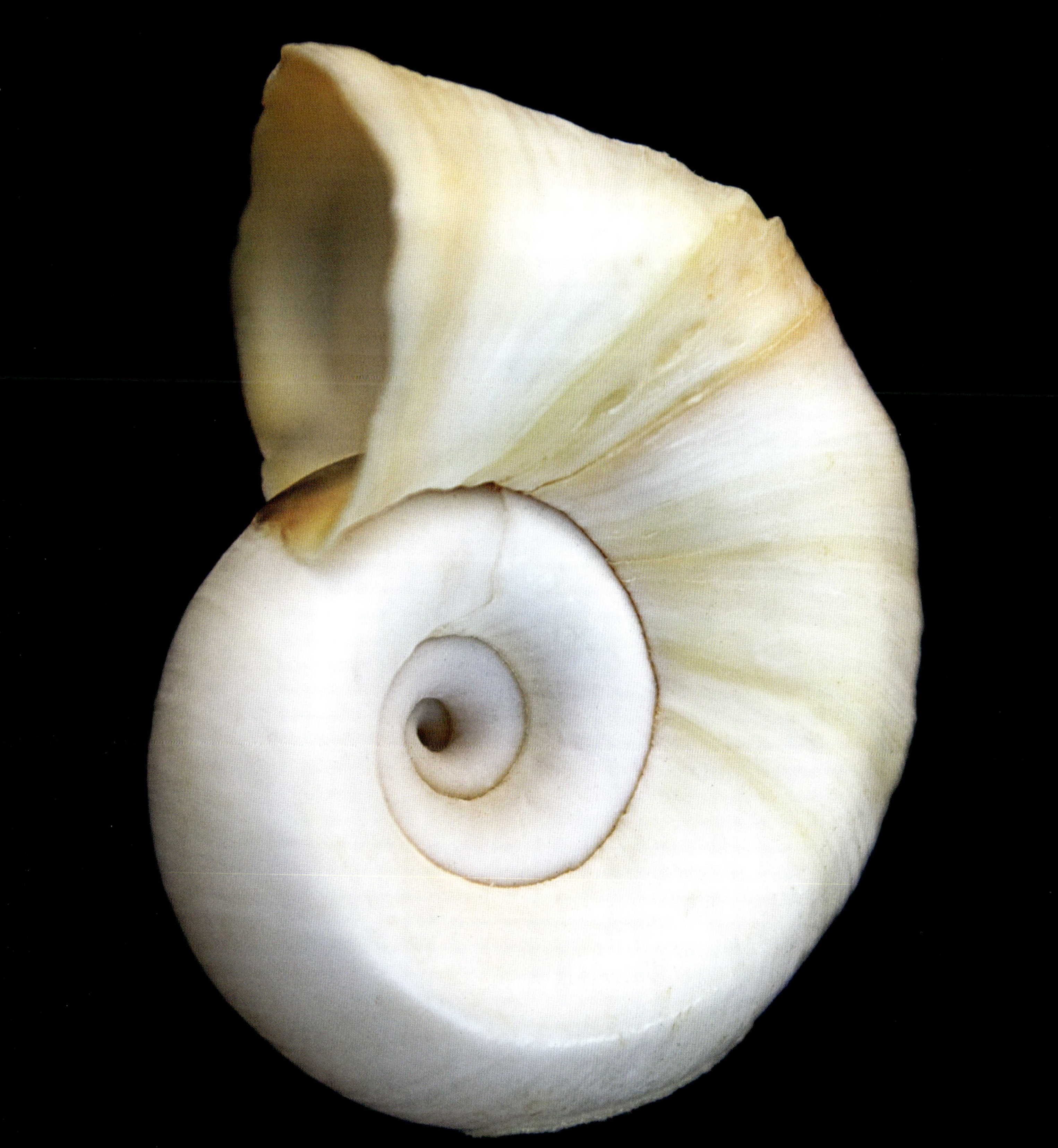

To think creatively, we must be able to look afresh at what we normally take for granted.

—Johann Wolfgang Von Goethe

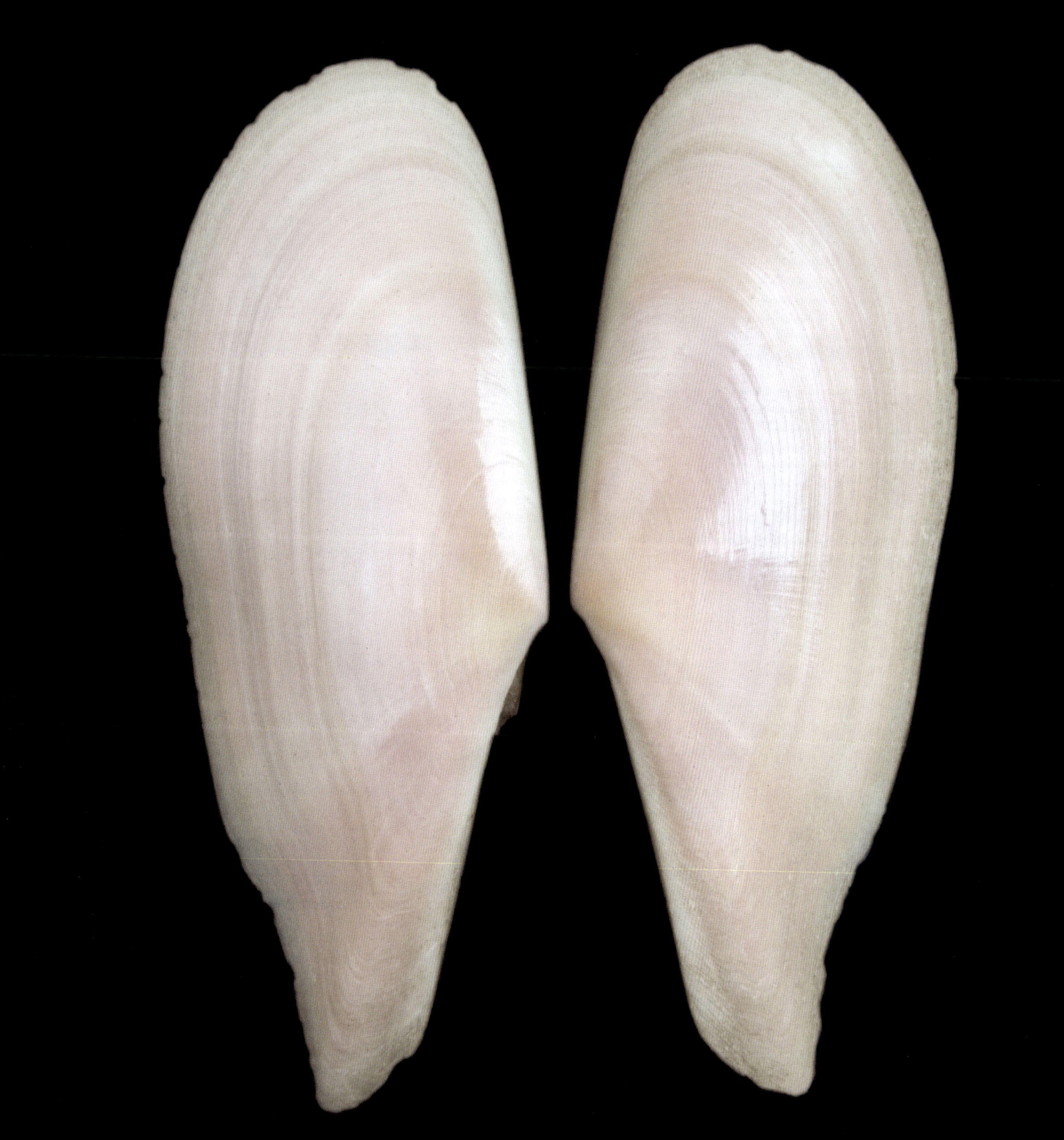

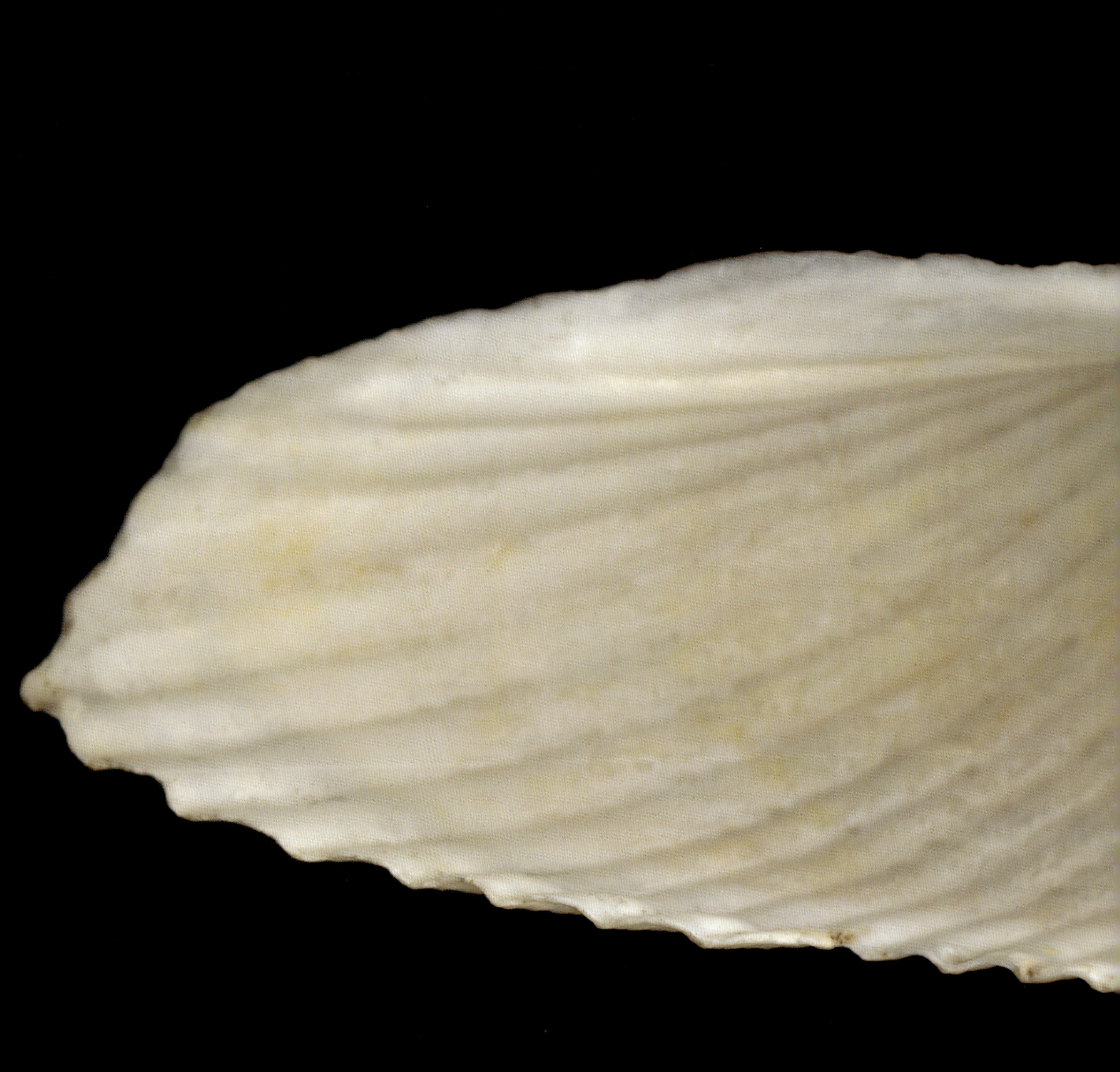

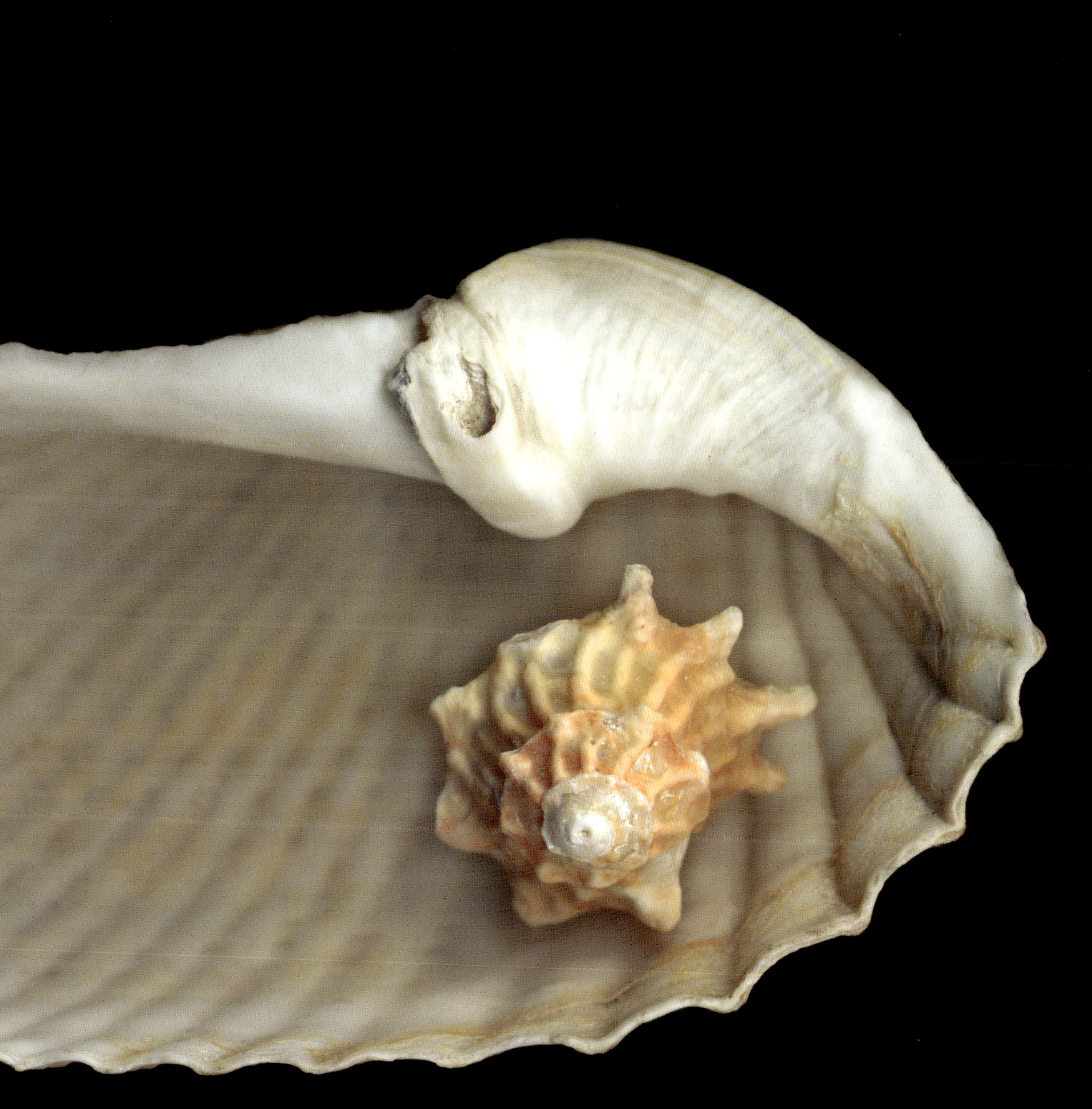

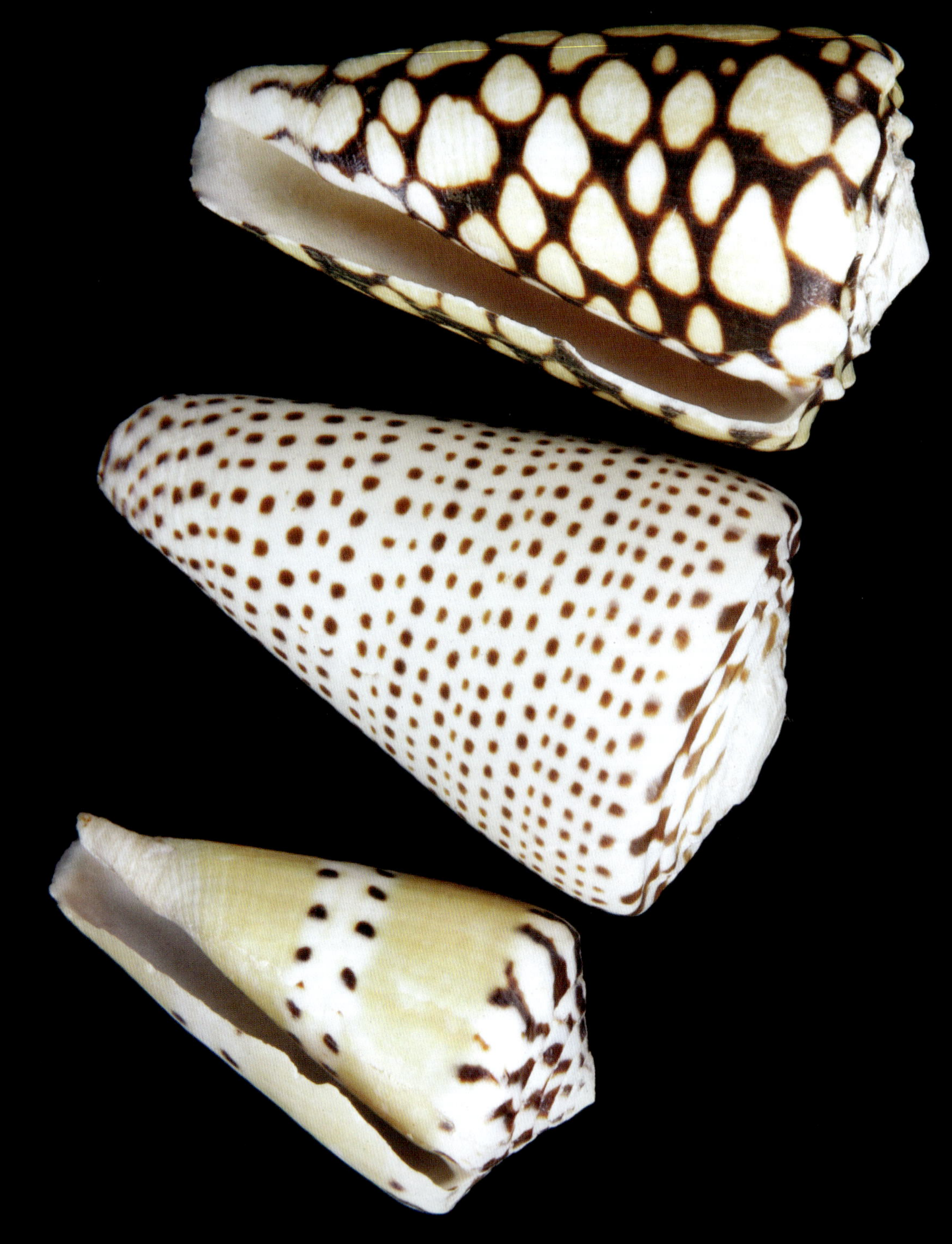

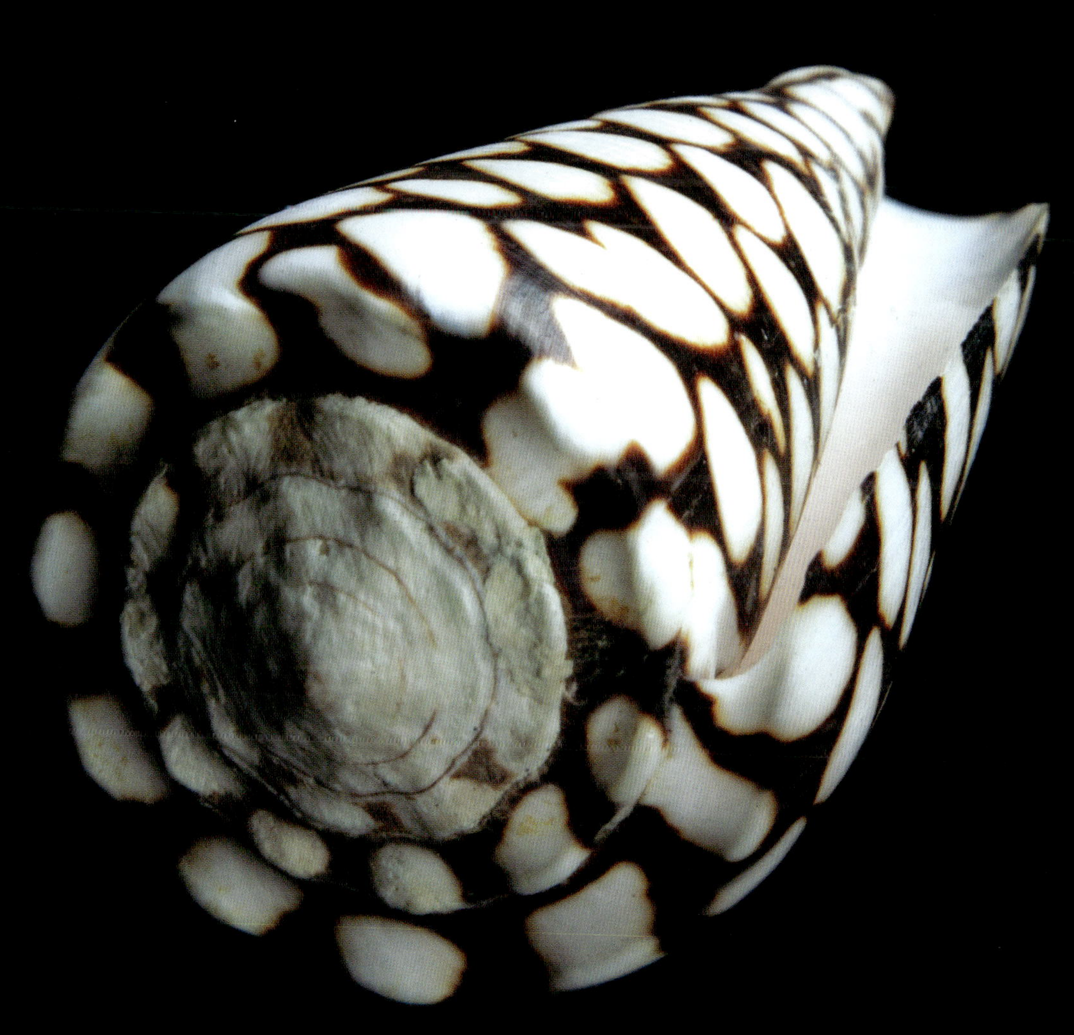

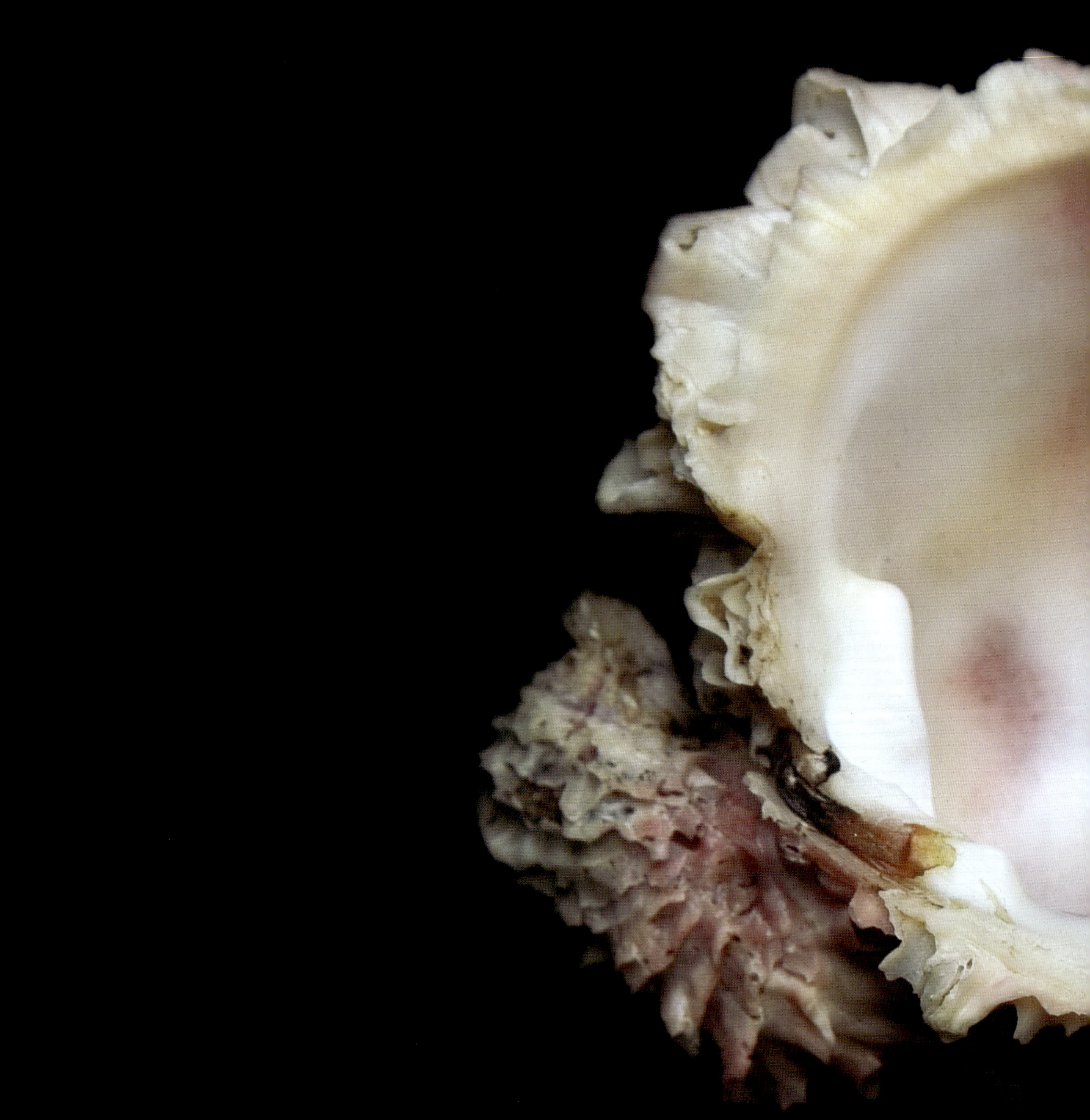

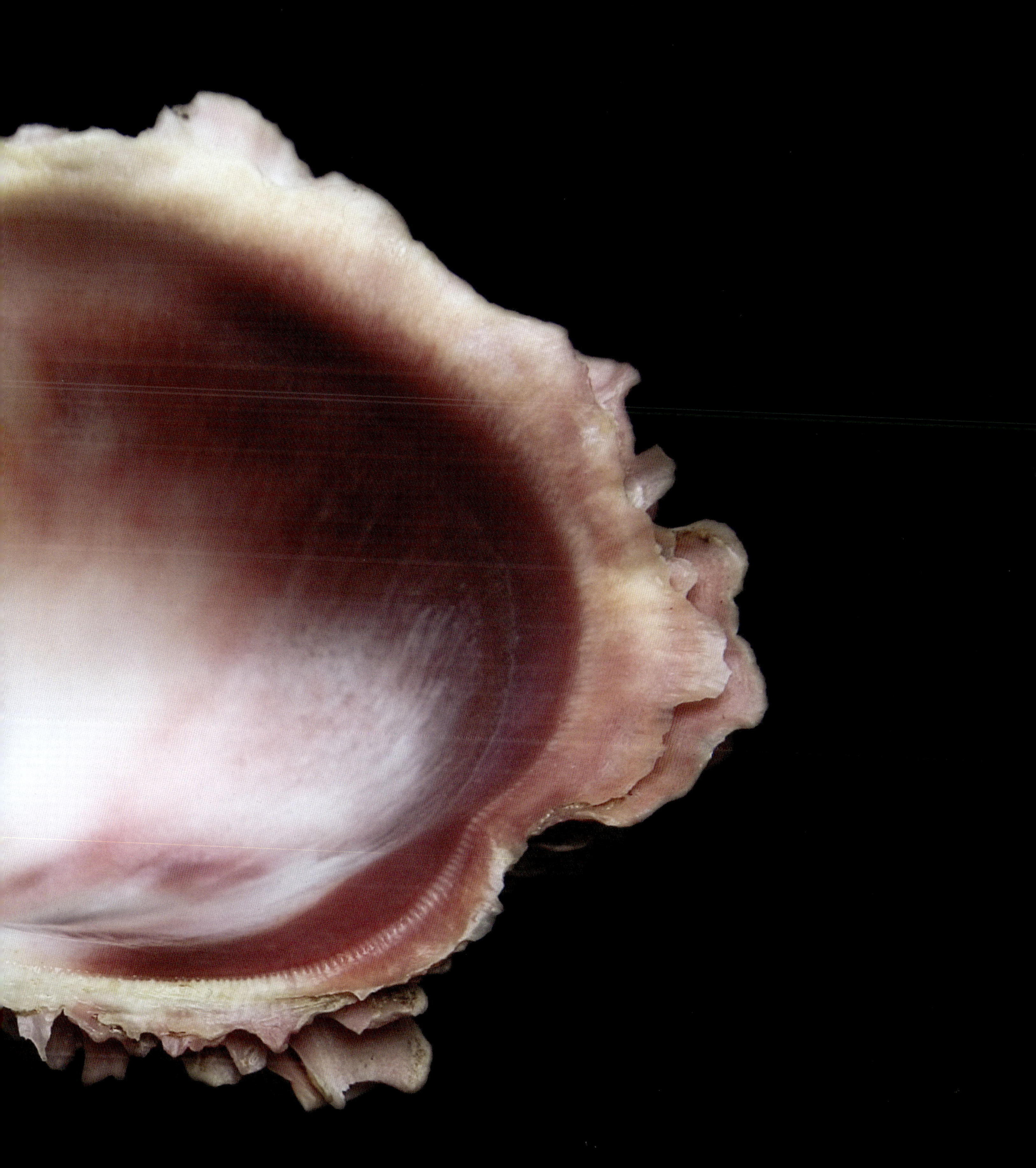

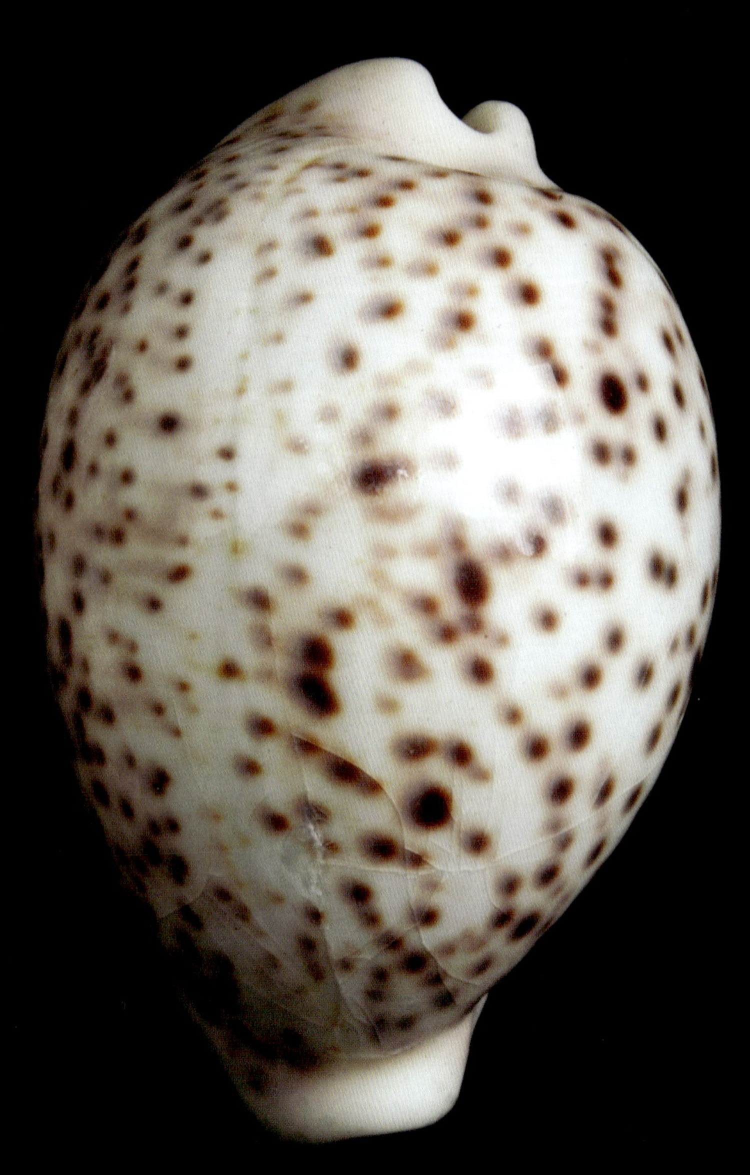

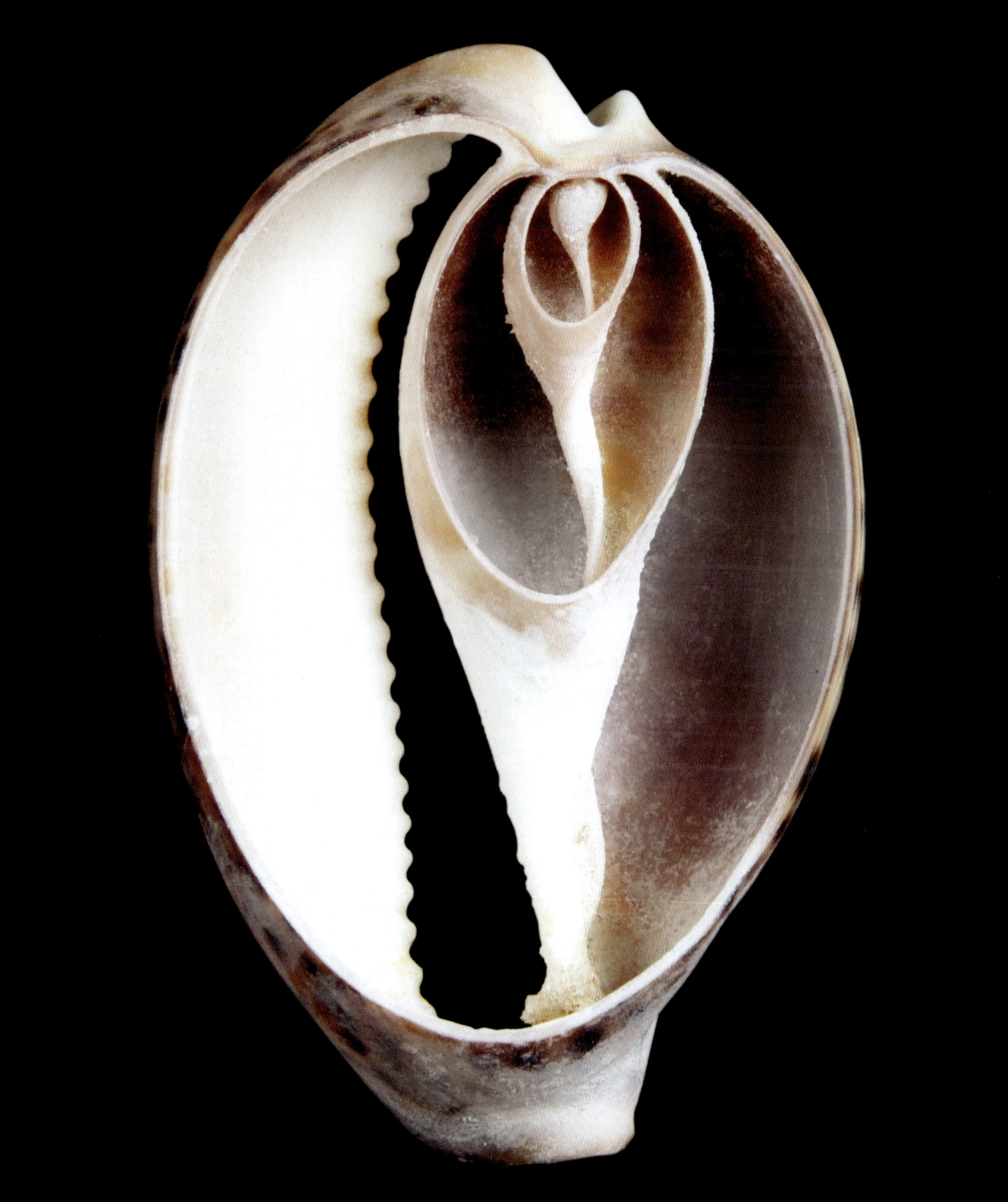

When you come to the One that gathers all things up into itself, there your soul must stay.

—Meister Eckhart

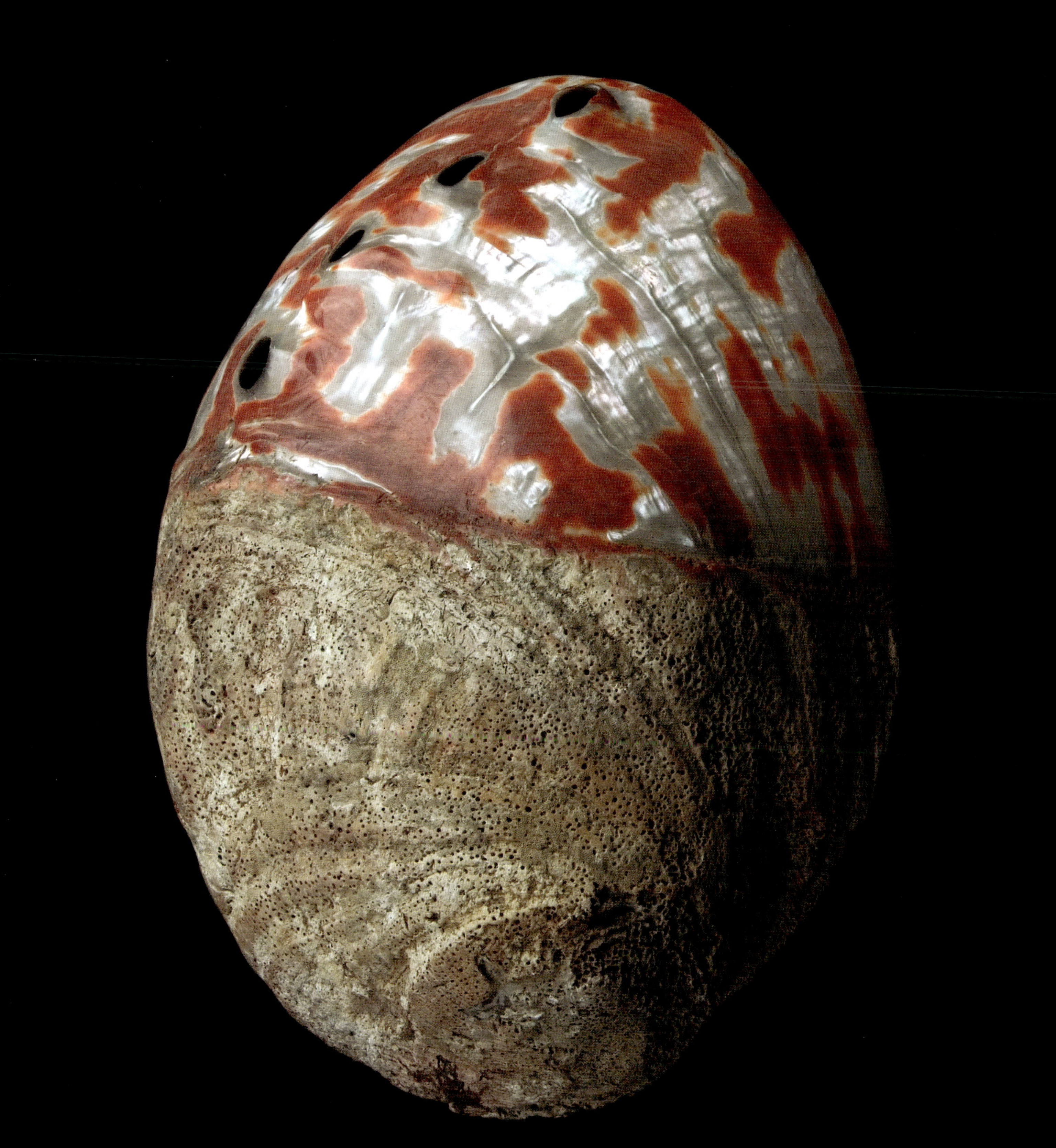

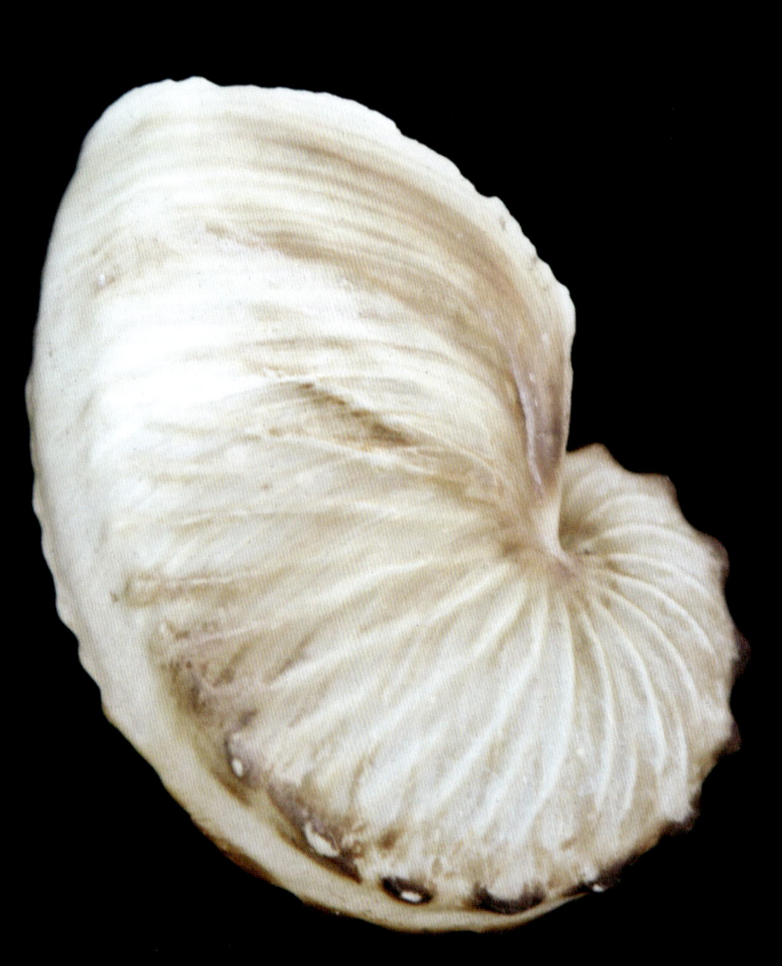

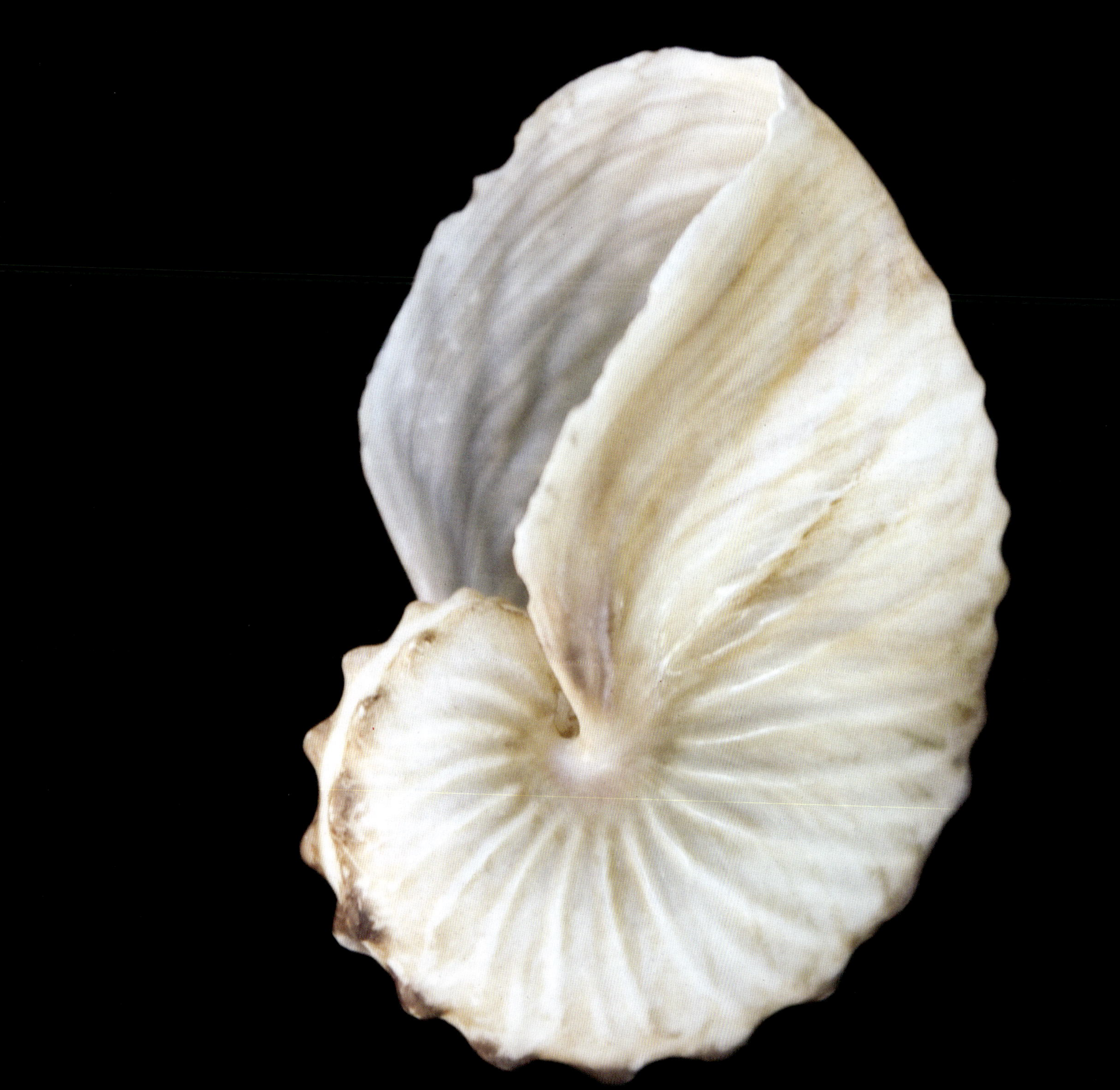

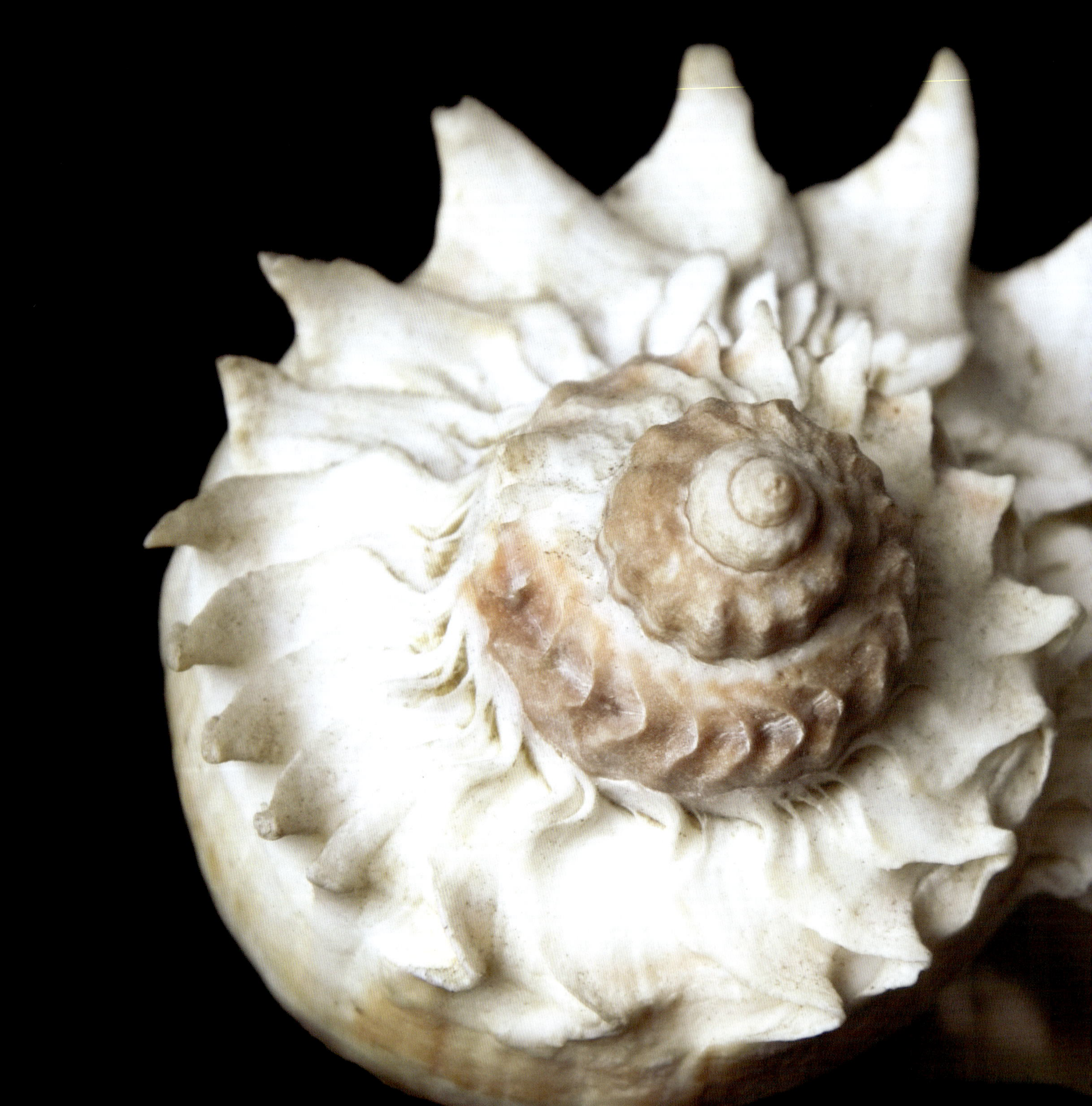

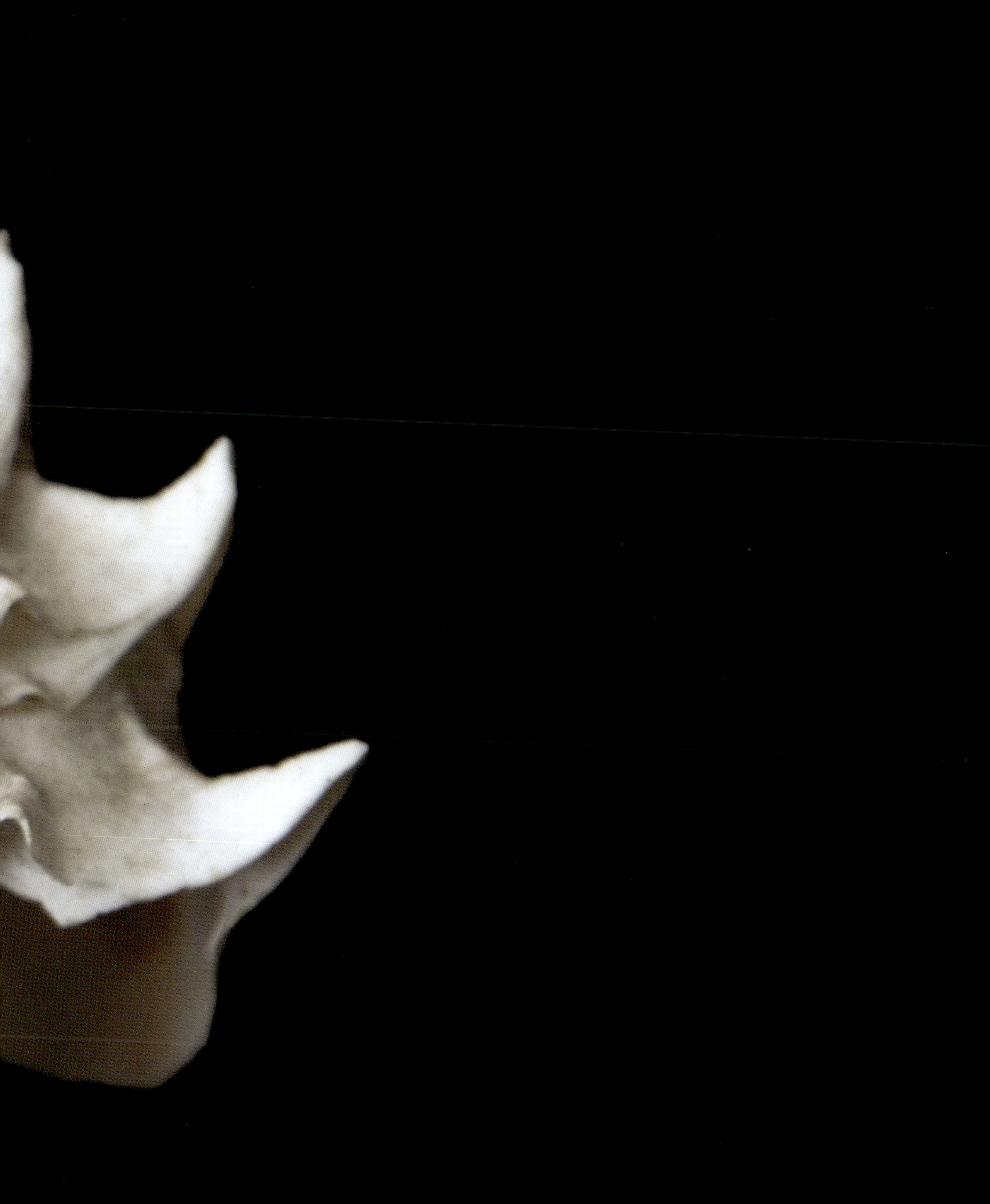

When I have a terrible need of —shall I say the word—religion. Then I go out and paint the stars.

—Vincent Van Gogh

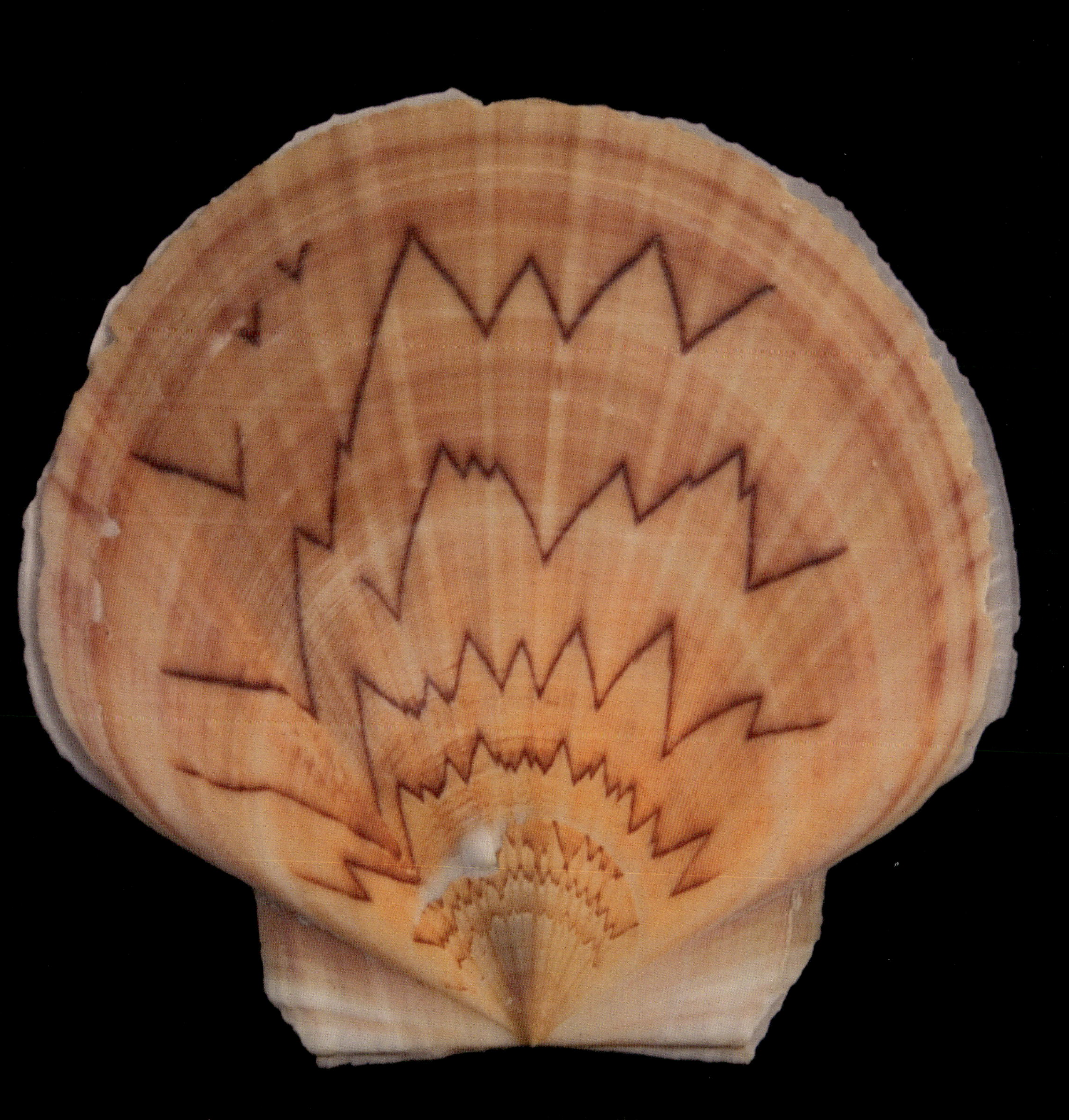

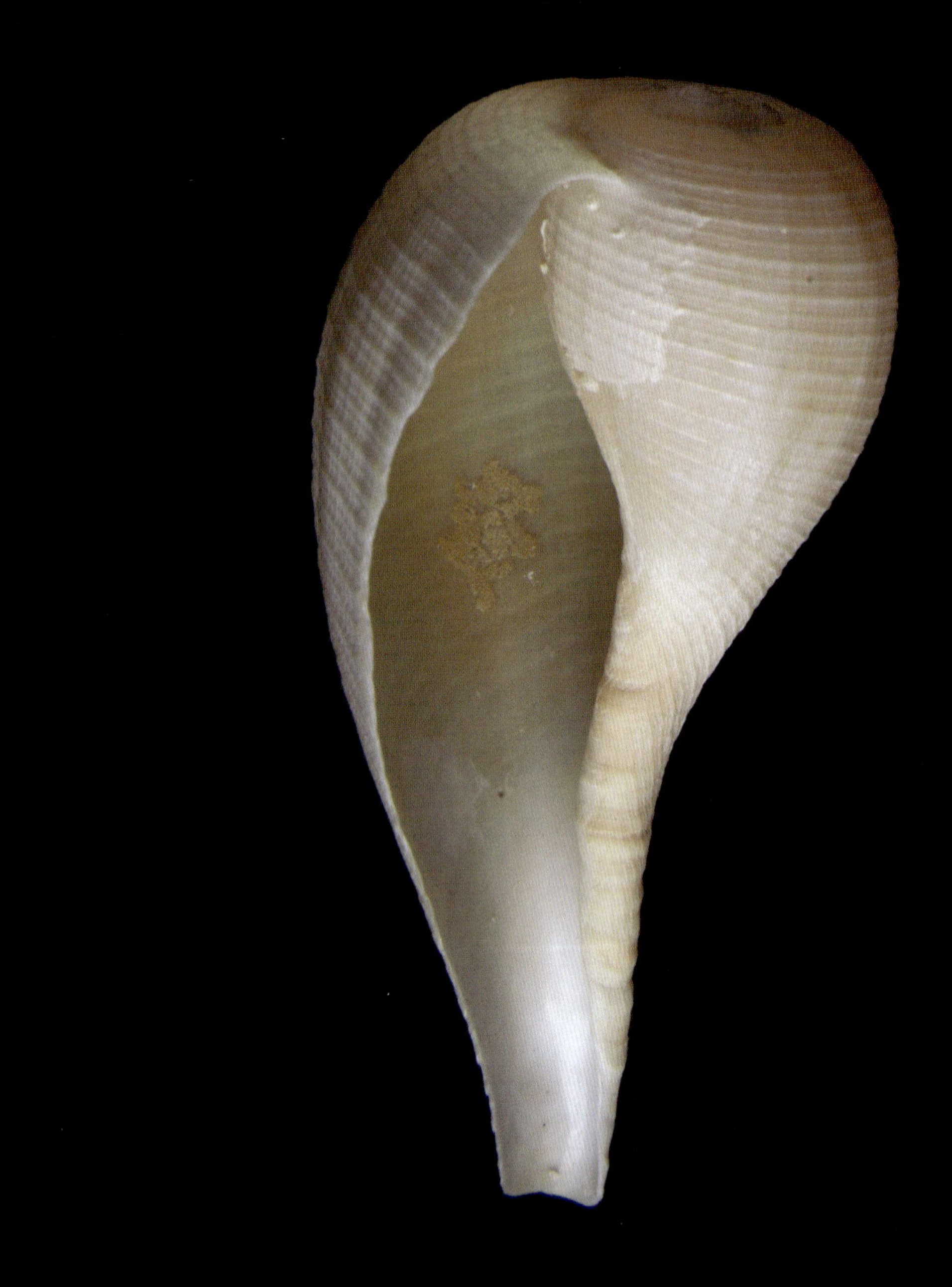

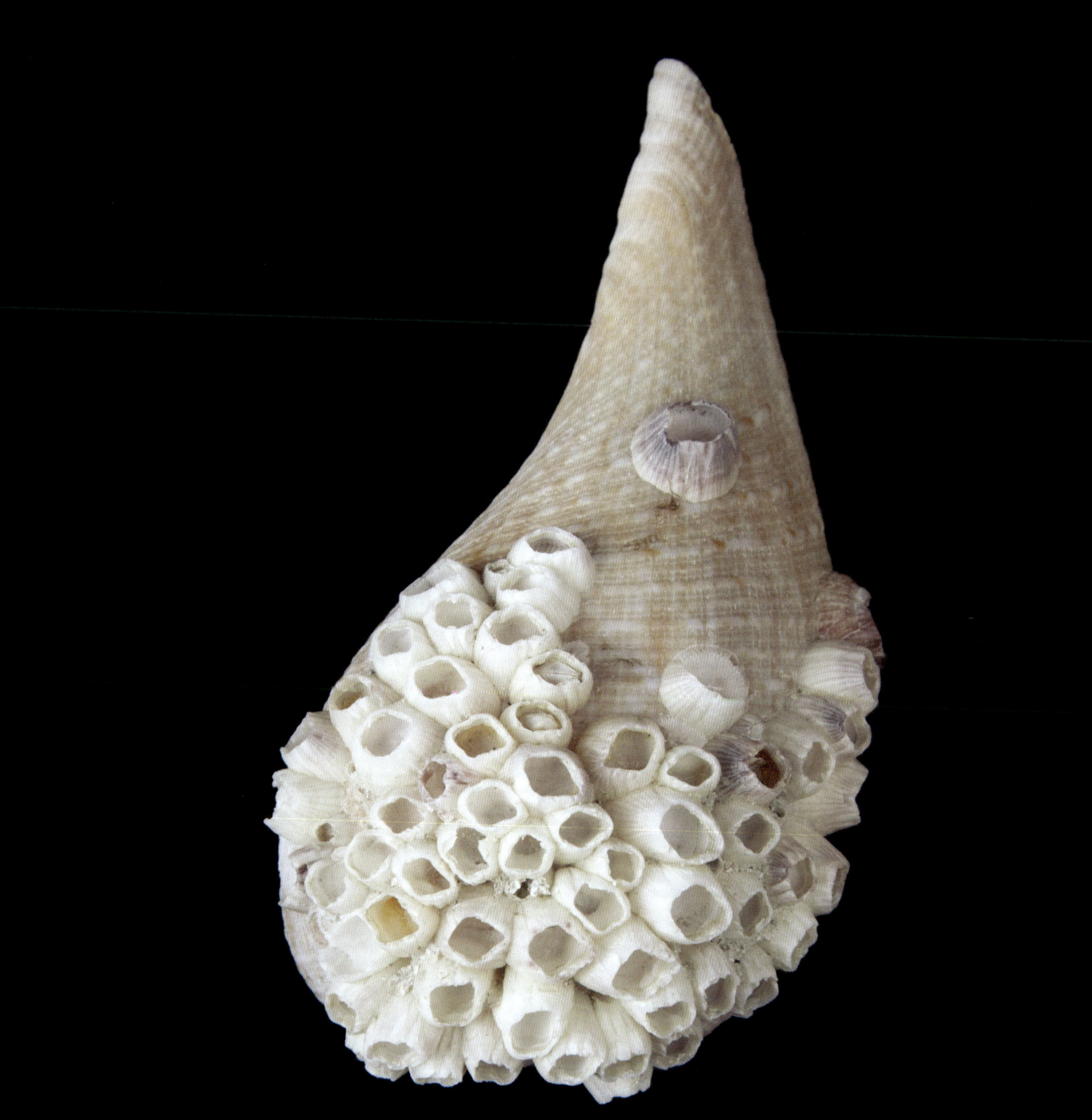

The voice of the sea speaks to the soul.

—Kate Chopin, *The Awakening*

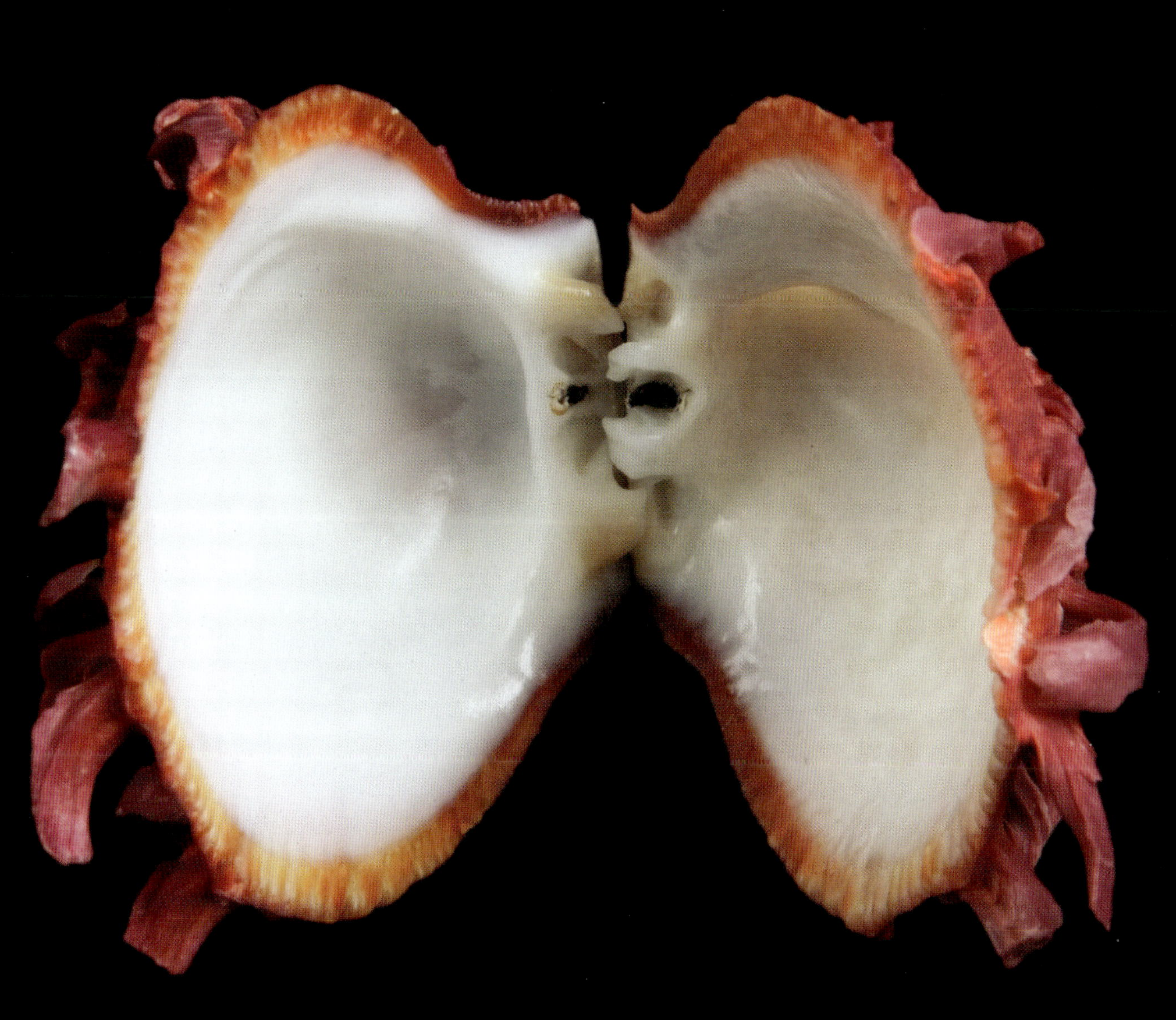

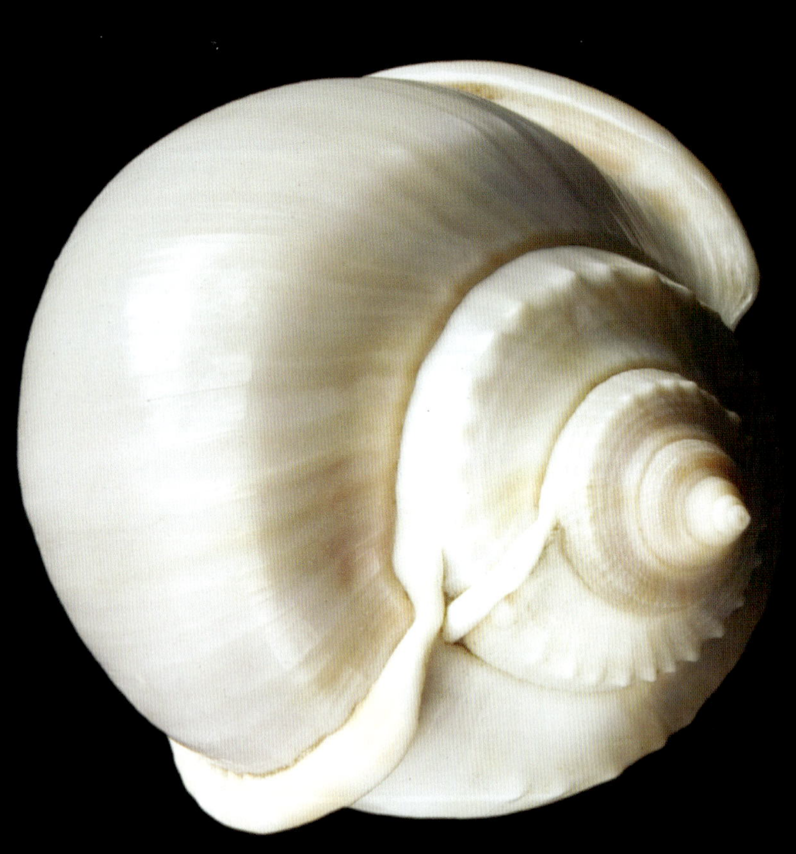

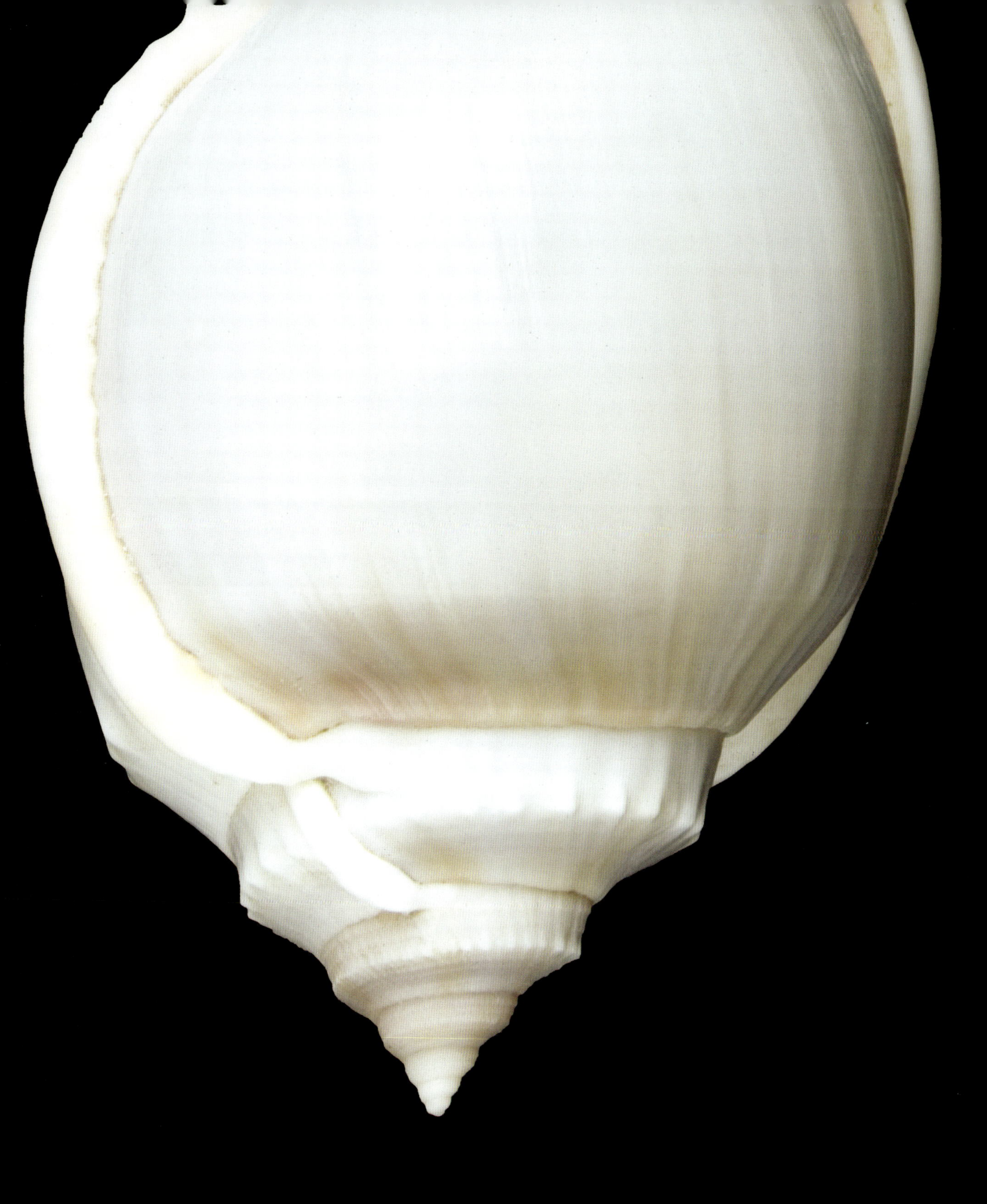

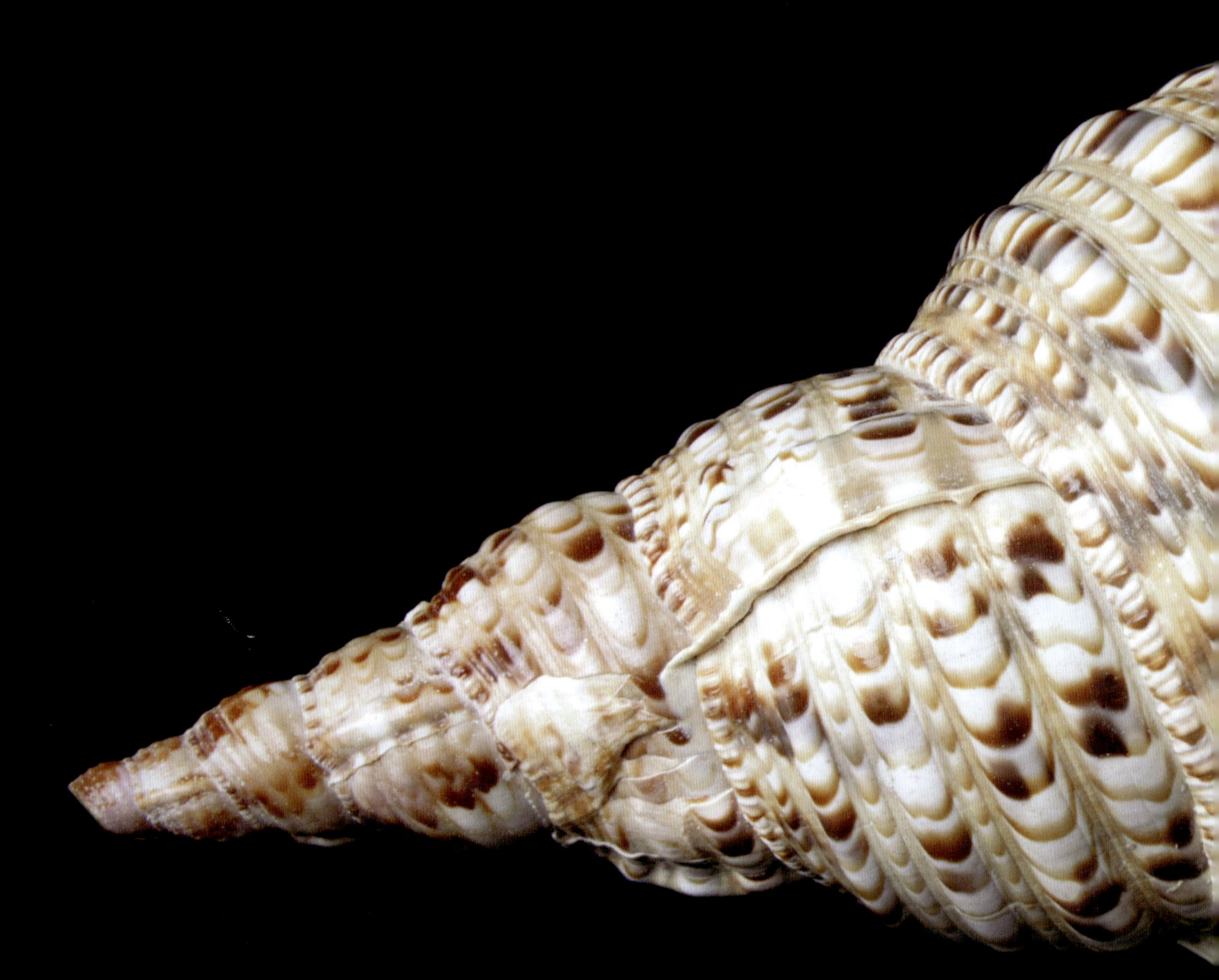

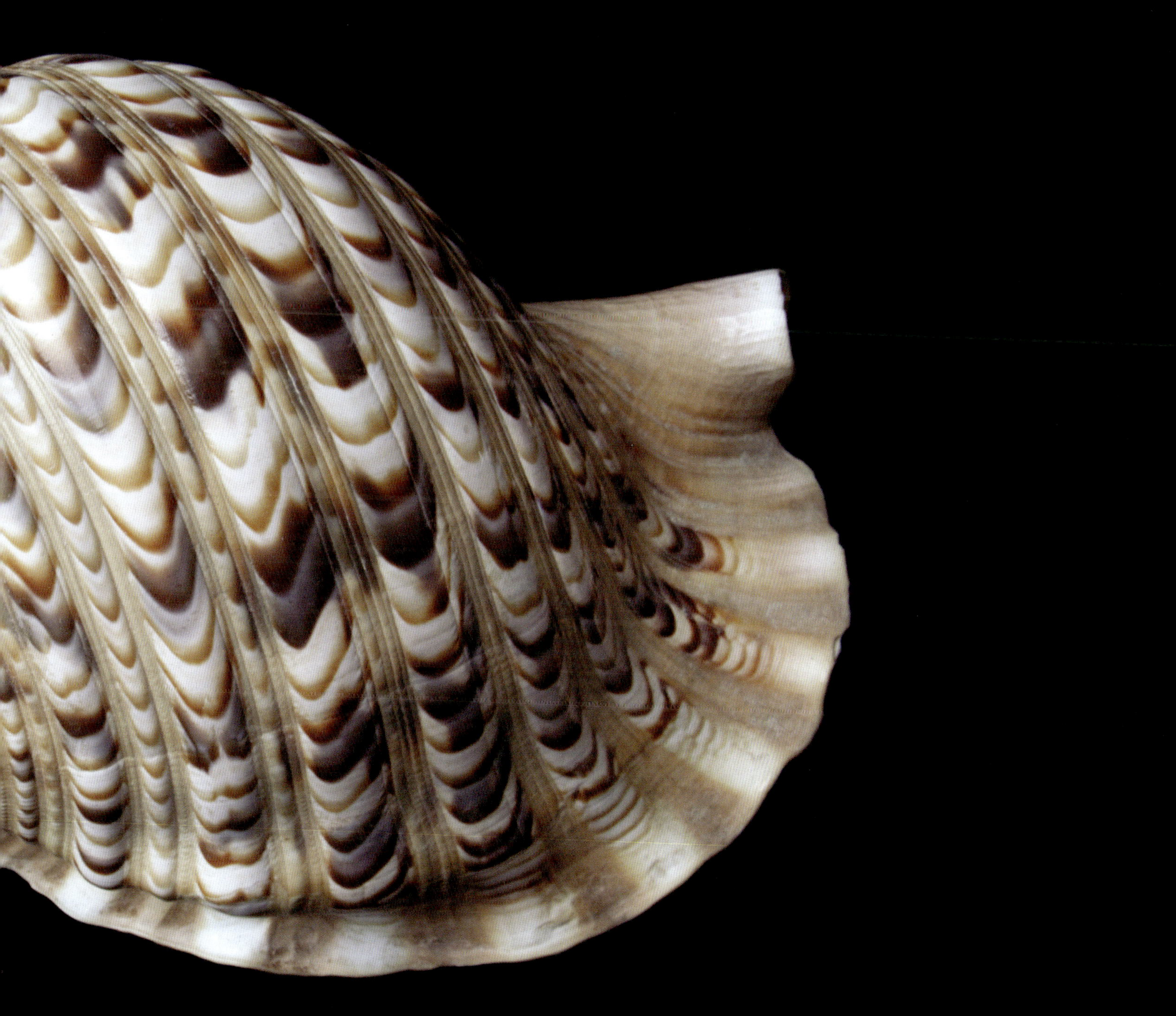

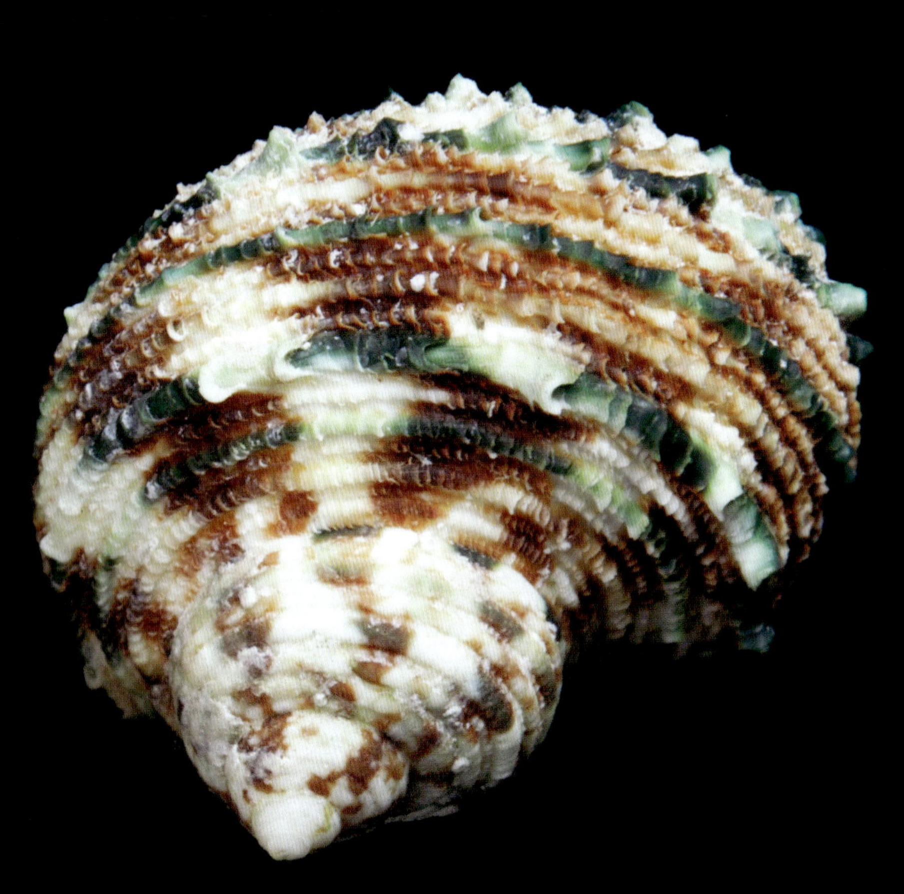

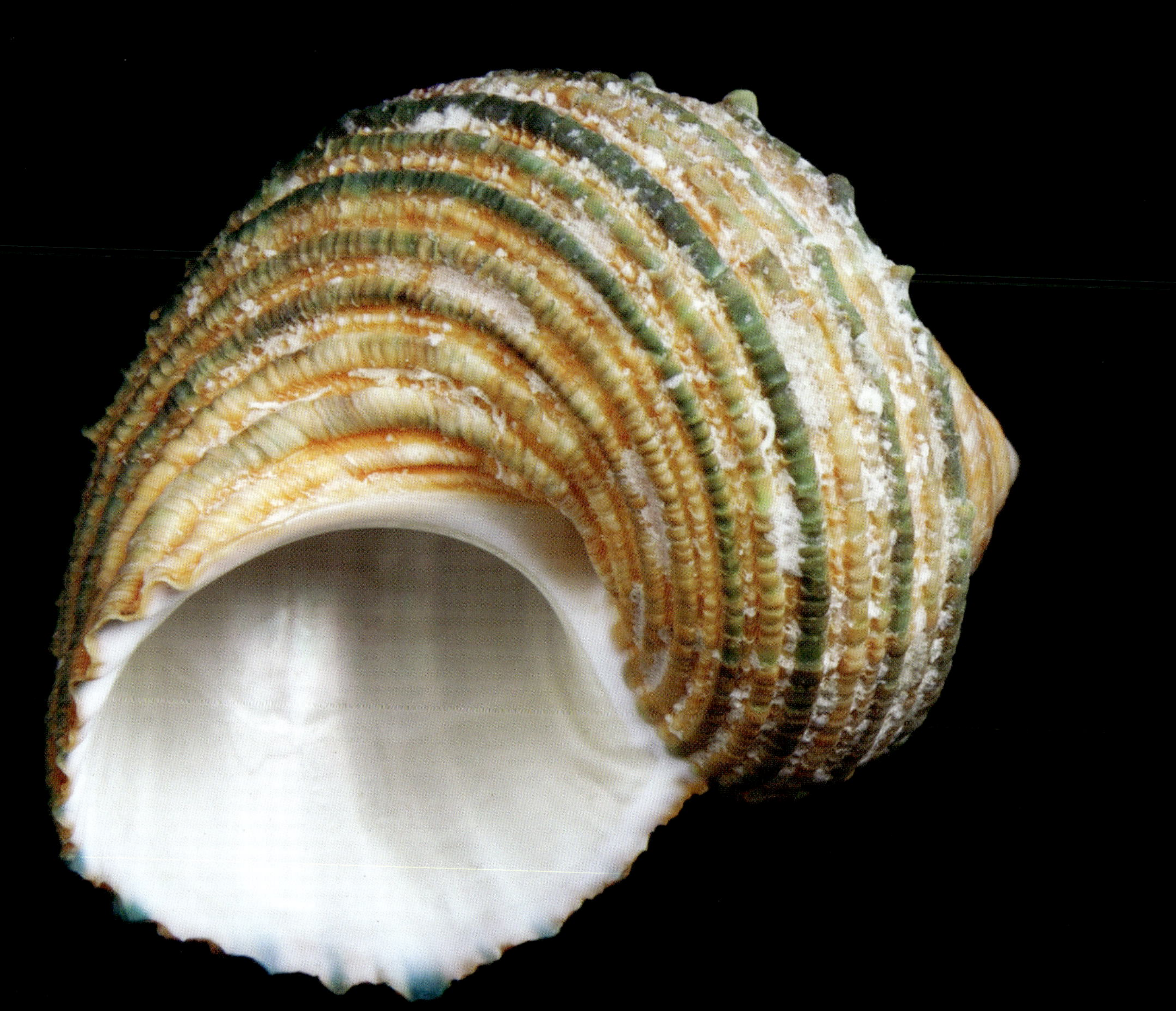

When the doors of perception are cleansed,
man will see things as they truly are, infinite.

—William Blake

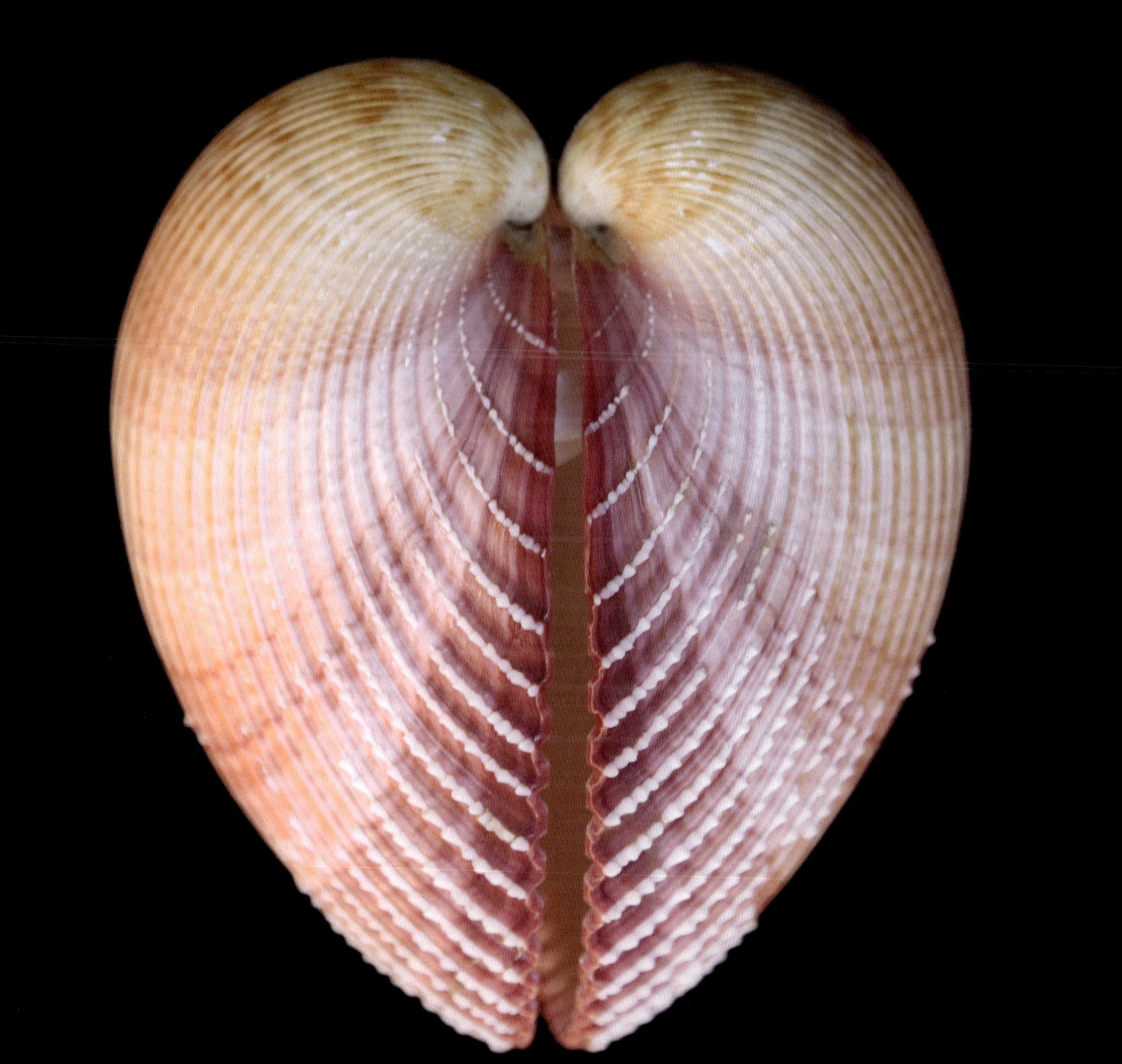

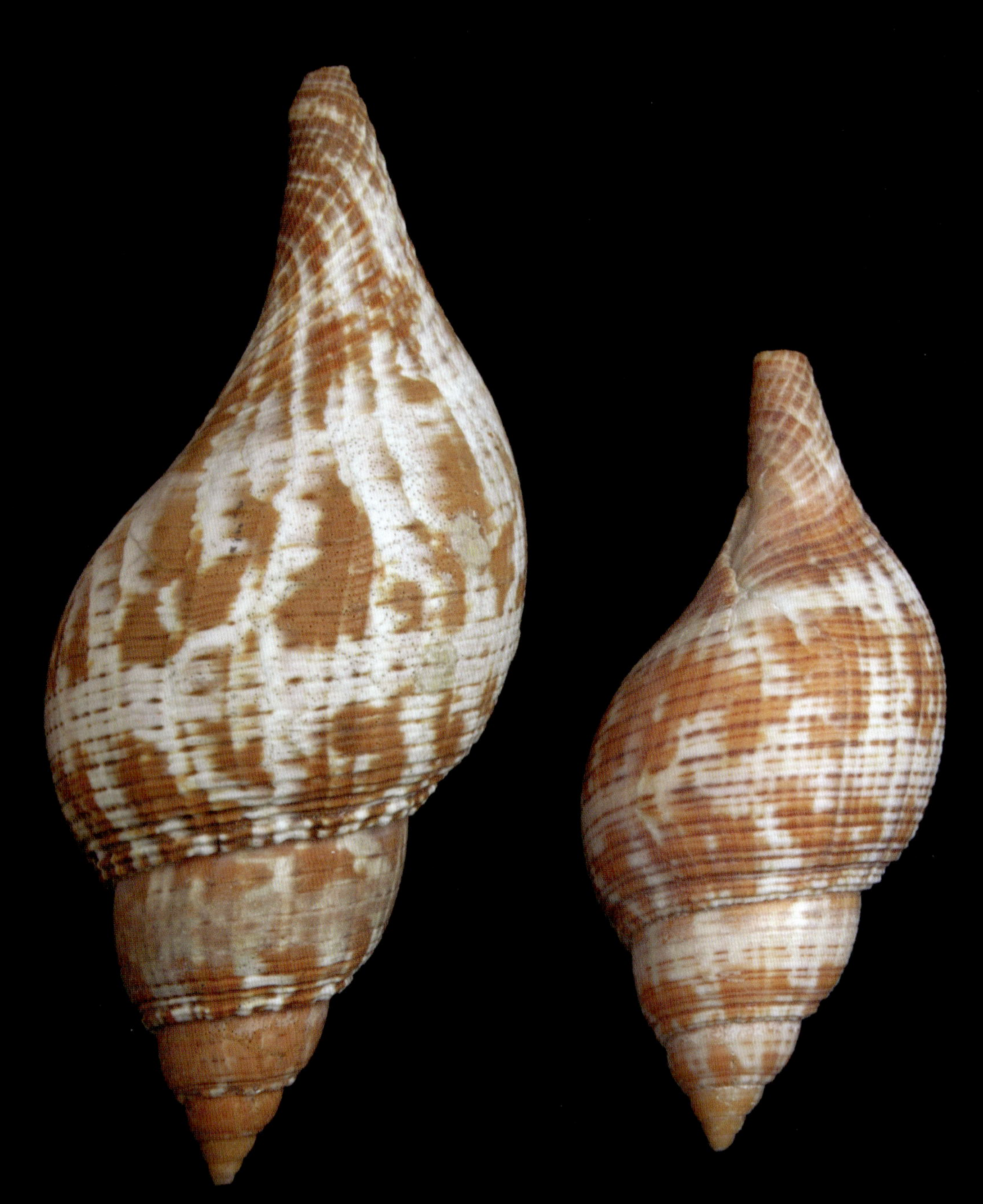

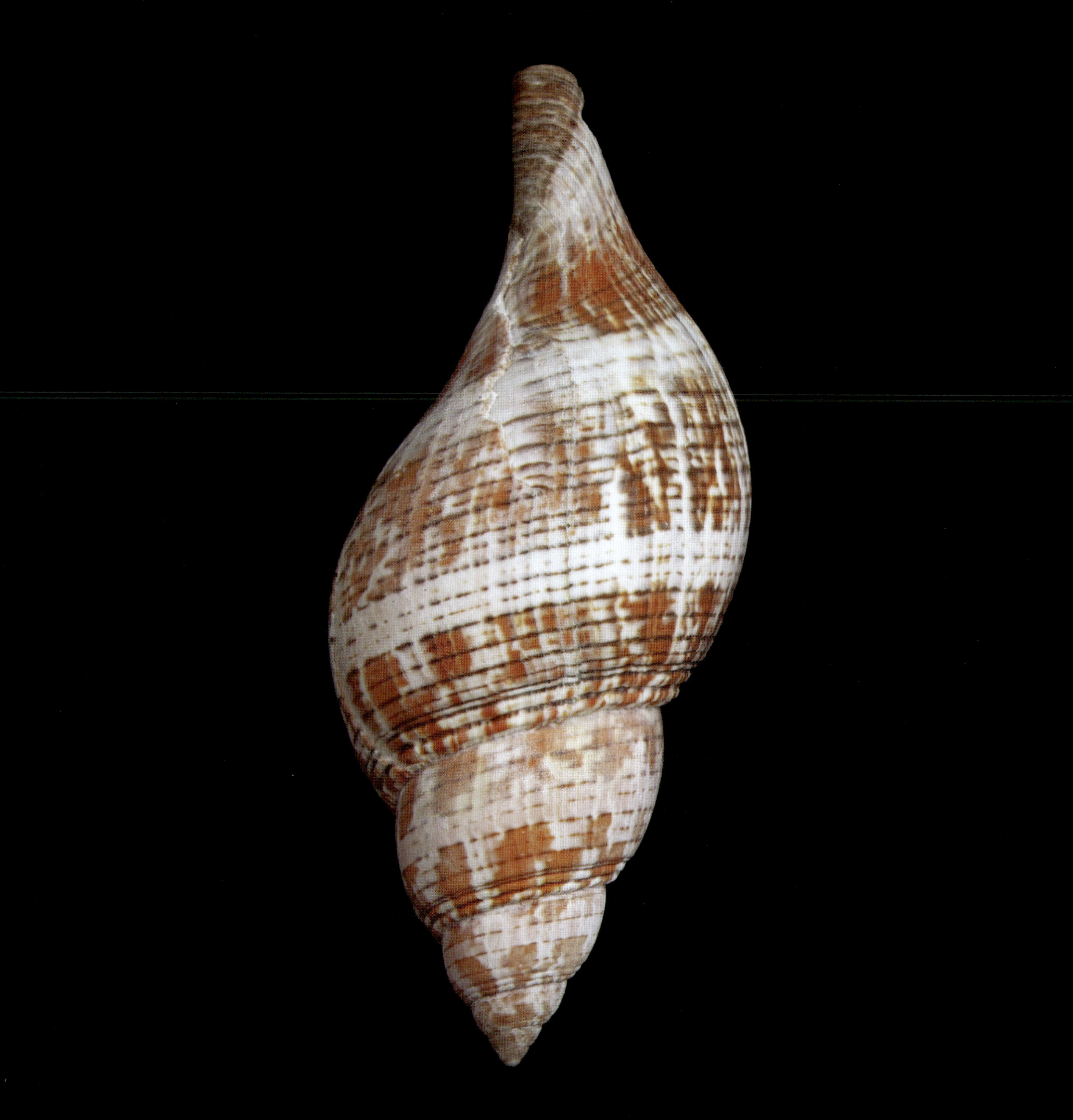

One who makes no mistakes makes nothing.

—Anonymous

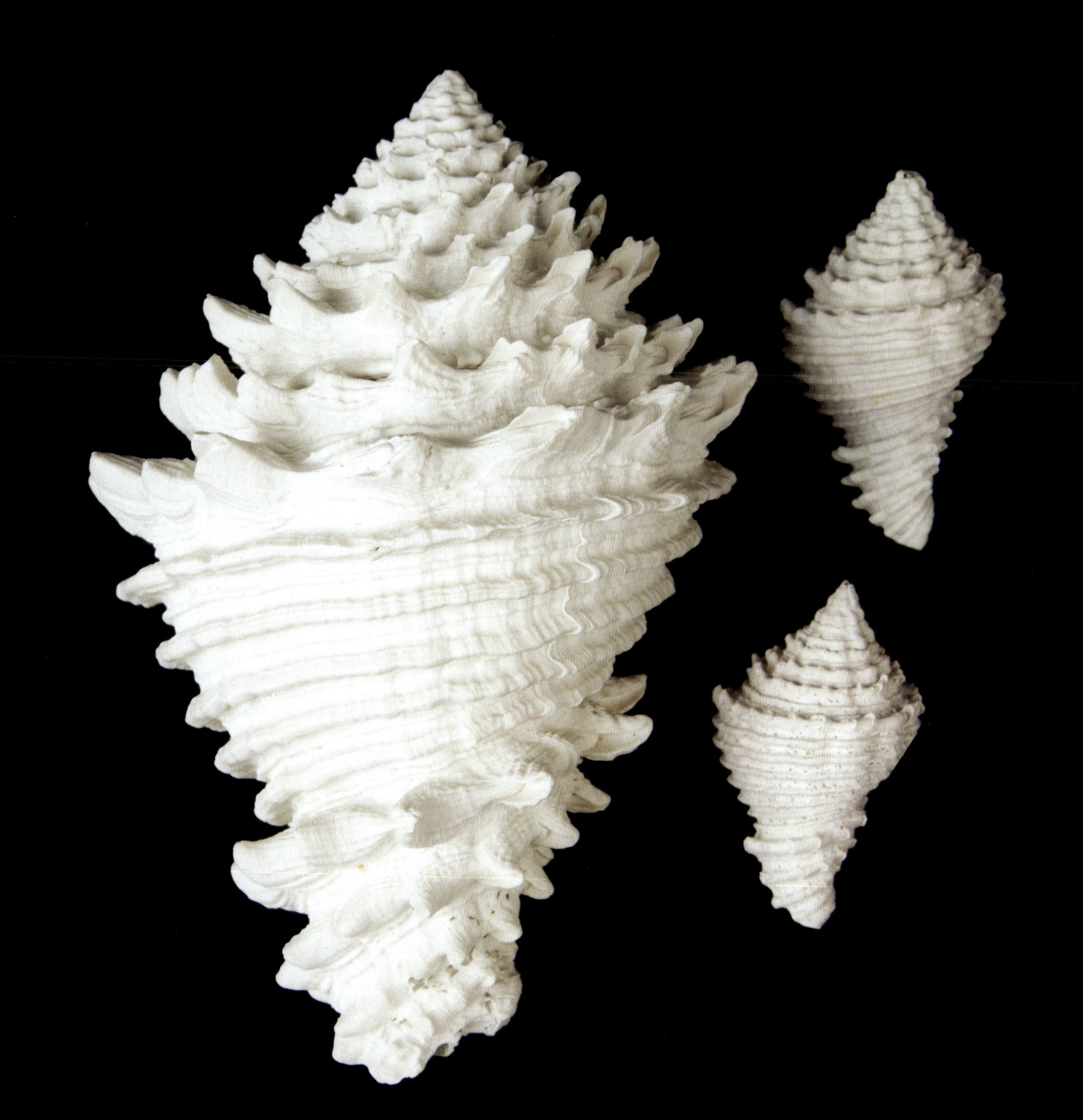

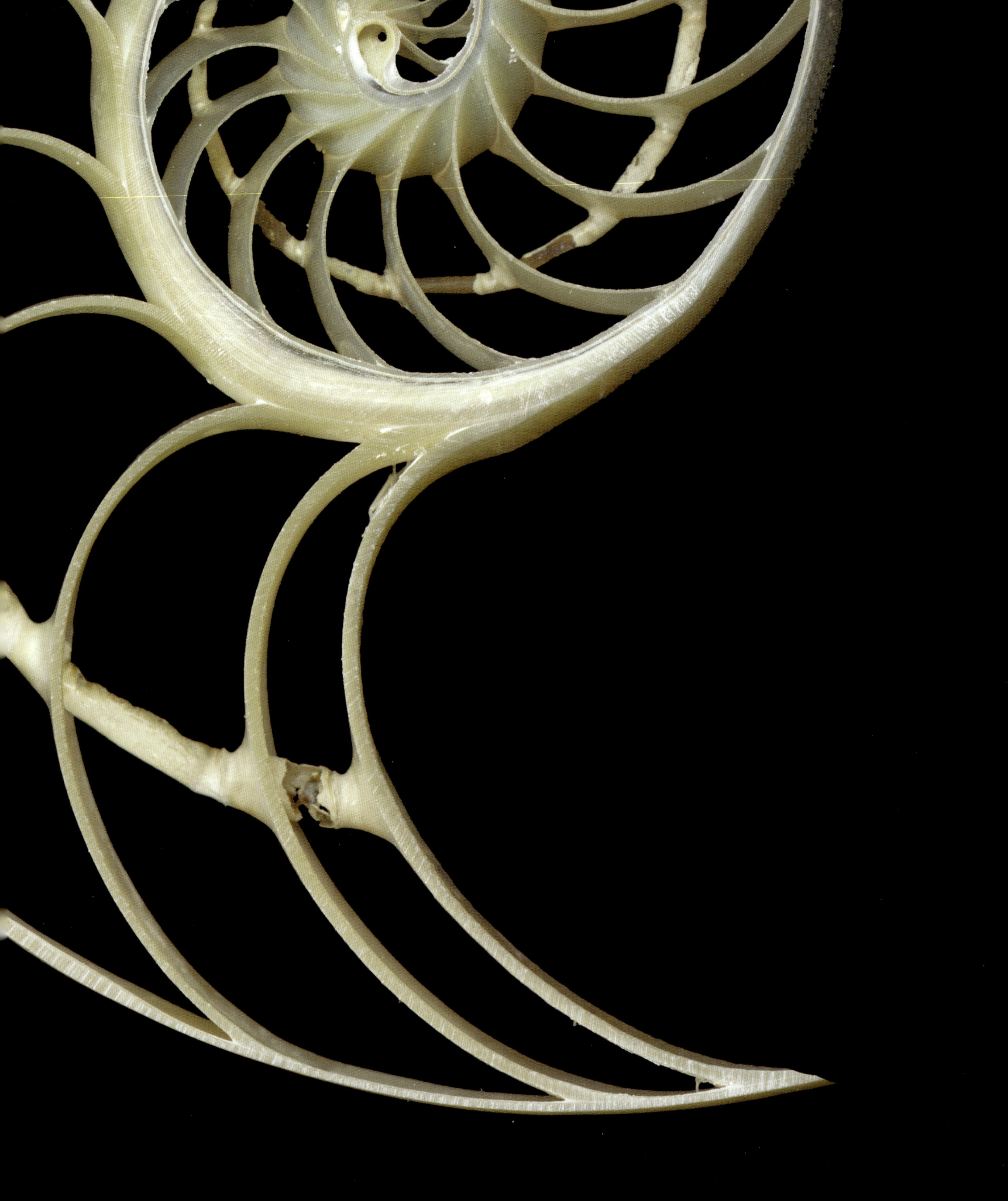

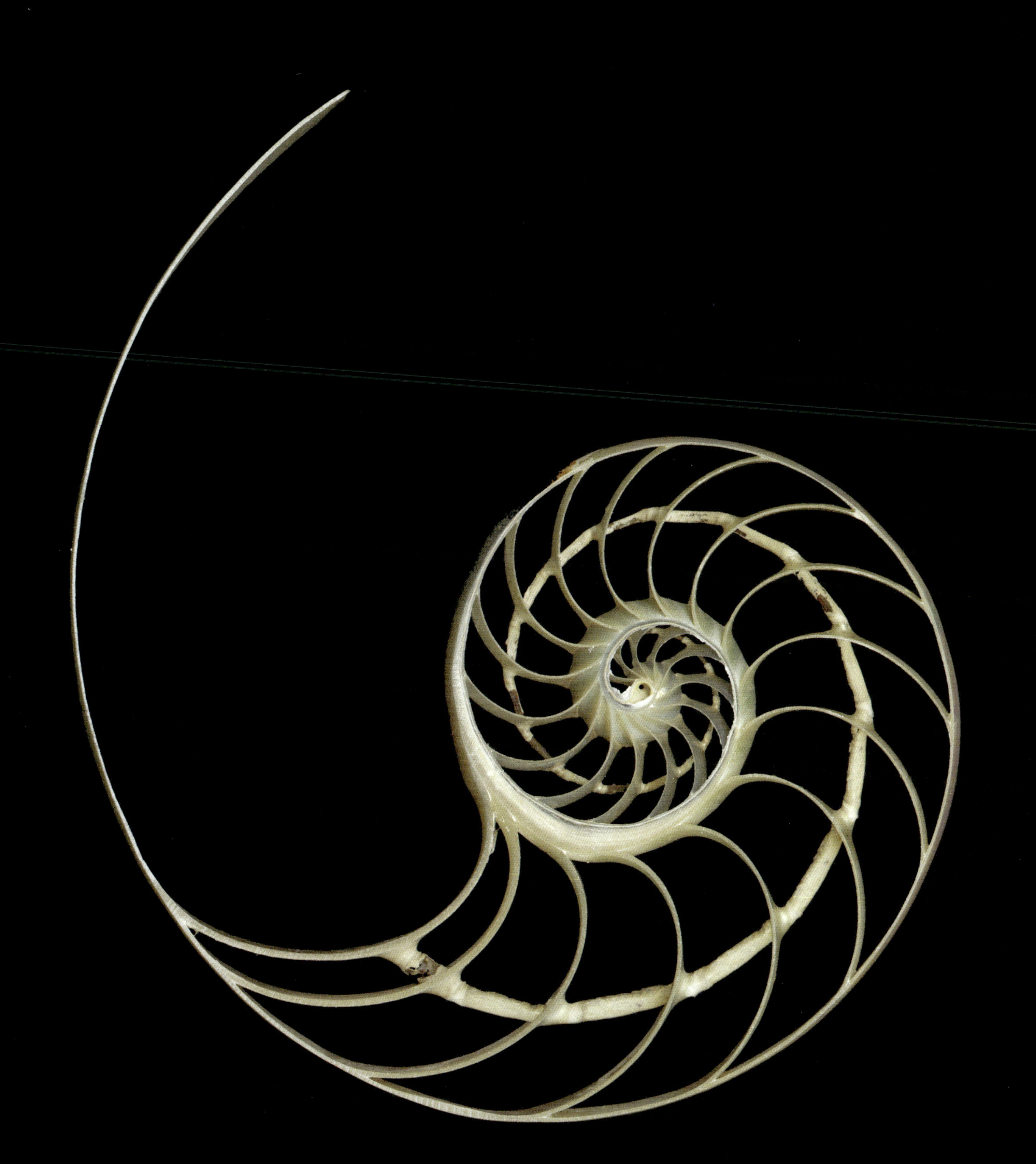

INDEX OF PLATES

ACKNOWLEDGMENTS

I would like to give special thanks to Thomas Cone and the Wentworth Shell Collection at Phillips Academy Andover, and to the research and secretarial work of Melanie Poulin and Ann Hamilton. I am grateful for having been able to photograph at the Bailey-Matthews Shell Museum in Sanibel, Florida. Their large archive was inspiring, and added greatly to my own personal collection of shells.

It was a pleasure working with Down East publishers on this book. I would particularly like to thank Michael Steere, Book Editor, and Miroslaw Jurek, Design Director.

In addition I would like to thank Matt Bagwell, who was the project manager and involved in all aspects of bringing this book to life.

A big thank you goes to Dowling Walsh Gallery in Rockland, Maine, who exhibits this work. For information on print sales of these images, please visit dowlingwalsh.com.

Finally, I am grateful to all the friends and family who have supported me throughout the years on my creative projects.